TABLE OF CONTENTS

TABLE OF CASES VII

TABLE OF AUTHORITIES IX

CHAPTER 1. NATURE AND SCOPE OF JUDICIAL REVIEW 1
2. *POLITICAL QUESTIONS* 1
   Rucho v. Common Cause 1
3. *CONGRESSIONAL REGULATION OF JUDICIAL POWER* 11

CHAPTER 2. NATIONAL LEGISLATIVE POWER 13
3. *THE NATIONAL TAXING AND SPENDING POWERS* 13
   I.   Regulation Through Taxing 13
        California v. Texas 13

CHAPTER 3. DISTRIBUTION OF FEDERAL POWERS:
SEPARATION OF POWERS 15
2. *CONGRESSIONAL ACTION AFFECTING "PRESIDENTIAL"*
   POWERS 15
   I.   Delegation of Rulemaking Power 15
        Gundy v. United States 15
   III. Appointment and Removal of Officers 16
        Seila Law LLC v. Consumer Financial Protection Bureau 16
        Collins v. Yellen 18
        United States v. Arthrex, Inc. 18
3. *EXECUTIVE PRIVILEGE AND IMMUNITY* 19
   Trump v. Vance 19
   Trump v. Mazars USA, LLP 22
4. *IMPEACHMENT OF THE PRESIDENT* 24

CHAPTER 4. STATE POWER TO REGULATE 27
2. *BASIC DOCTRINAL PRINCIPLES AND THEIR APPLICATION 27*
   I.   Statutes That Discriminate on Their Faces Against Interstate
        Commerce 27
        Tennessee Wine and Spirits Retailers Ass'n v. Tennessee Alcoholic
        Beverage Comm'n 27

CHAPTER 5. SUBSTANTIVE PROTECTION OF ECONOMIC
INTERESTS 29
4. *OTHER LIMITS ON ECONOMIC LEGISLATION: THE*
   PROHIBITION AGAINST "TAKING" "PRIVATE PROPERTY"
   WITHOUT JUST COMPENSATION 29
   Cedar Point Nursery v. Hasid 29

CHAPTER 6. PROTECTION OF INDIVIDUAL RIGHTS: DUE PROCESS, THE BILL OF RIGHTS, AND UNENUMERATED RIGHTS 31

1. *APPLICABILITY OF THE BILL OF RIGHTS TO THE STATES; NATURE AND SCOPE OF FOURTEENTH AMENDMENT DUE PROCESS* 31

    II. Is the Bill of Rights Incorporated "Jot-for-Jot"? 31

    III. In *McDonald v. City of Chicago*, the Court Looks Back on Its "Incorporation" of Bill of Rights Guarantees 31

        Timbs v. Indiana 31

        Ramos v. Louisiana 32

    IV. How Much More Specific Are Provisions of the Bill of Rights than Due Process Generally? The Case of Bodily Extractions 33

        Jacobson v. Massachusetts 33

2. *REPRODUCTIVE FREEDOM* 34

    Introductory Note on the Right of "Privacy" 34

    The Court Reaffirms "the Essential Holding of *Roe*" 34

        Dobbs v. Jackson Women's Health 34

    Purported Health Regulations 35

        June Medical Services L. L. C. v. Russo 35

7. *THE RIGHT TO KEEP AND BEAR ARMS* 40

    New York State Rifle & Pistol Ass'n v. City of New York 40

    New York State Rifle v. Corlett 41

8. *THE DEATH PENALTY AND RELATED PROBLEMS: CRUEL AND UNUSUAL PUNISHMENT* 41

    IV. Additional Constitutional Limits on Imposing Severe Punishment 41

        Ford v. Wainwright 41

        Madison v. Alabama 41

        Jones v. Missisippi 41

        Bucklew v. Precythe 42

CHAPTER 7. FREEDOM OF EXPRESSION AND ASSOCIATION 43

1. *THE SCOPE AND STRENGTH OF THE FIRST AMENDMENT* 43

    I. Advocacy of Illegal Action 43

        D. A Modern "Restatement" 43

            Nieves v. Bartlett 43

    II. Reputation and Privacy 44

        B. Public Officials and Seditious Libel 44

2. *THE PROBLEM OF CONTENT REGULATION* 45

    Iancu v. Brunetti 45

    I. "Hate Speech" and the *Skokie* Controversy 45

        Barr v. American Association of Political Consultants, Inc. 45

4. *NEW CATEGORIES?* 47

    I. Harm to Children and the Overbreadth Doctrine 47

2021 SUPPLEMENT TO
CONSTITUTIONAL LAW
CASES, COMMENTS, AND QUESTIONS

Thirteenth Edition

■ ■ ■

Jesse H. Choper
Earl Warren Professor of Public Law (Emeritus)
University of California, Berkeley

Michael C. Dorf
Robert S. Stevens Professor of Law
Cornell University

Richard H. Fallon, Jr.
Story Professor of Law
Harvard University

Frederick Schauer
David and Mary Harrison Distinguished Professor of Law
University of Virginia

AMERICAN CASEBOOK SERIES®

WEST
ACADEMIC
PUBLISHING

American Casebook Series is a trademark registered in the U.S. Patent and Trademark Office.

© 2020 LEG, Inc. d/b/a West Academic
© 2021 LEG, Inc. d/b/a West Academic
    444 Cedar Street, Suite 700
    St. Paul, MN 55101
    1-877-888-1330

West, West Academic Publishing, and West Academic are trademarks of West Publishing Corporation, used under license.

Printed in the United States of America

ISBN: 978-1-64708-888-0

7. *GOVERNMENT SPEECH* 48
    II.   Government as Educator and Editor 48
        Mahanoy Area School District v. B. L. 48
9. *THE RIGHT NOT TO SPEAK, THE RIGHT TO ASSOCIATE, AND*
    THE RIGHT NOT TO ASSOCIATE 58
    I.   The Right Not to Be Associated with Particular Ideas 58
10. *WEALTH, EQUALITY, AND THE POLITICAL PROCESS* 60

CHAPTER 8. FREEDOM OF RELIGION 61
1. *THE ESTABLISHMENT CLAUSE* 61
    IV. Official Acknowledgment of Religion 61
        American Legion v. American Humanist Ass'n 61
2. *THE FREE EXERCISE CLAUSE AND RELATED STATUTORY*
    ISSUES 62
    I.   Conflict with State Regulation 62
        Espinoza v. Montana Department of Revenue 63
        Fulton v. City of Philadelphia 66
        South Bay Pentecostal Church v. Newsom 68
        Tandon v. Newsom 68

CHAPTER 9. EQUAL PROTECTION 71
2. *RACE AND ETHNIC ANCESTRY* 71
    IV. De Jure vs. De Facto Discrimination 71
        Department of Homeland Security v. Regents of University of
            California 71
4. *SPECIAL SCRUTINY FOR OTHER CLASSIFICATIONS:*
    DOCTRINE AND DEBATES 71
    I.   Sexual Orientation 71
5. *FUNDAMENTAL RIGHTS* 72
    I.   Voting 72
        D.   "Dilution" of the Right: Partisan Gerrymanders 72
        Davis v. Bandemer 72

CHAPTER 10. THE CONCEPT OF STATE ACTION 75
2. *"GOVERNMENT FUNCTION"* 75
    III. Refusals to Find "Governmental Function" 75
        Manhattan Community Access Corp. v. Halleck 75

CHAPTER 12. LIMITATIONS ON JUDICIAL POWER AND
    REVIEW 77
2. *STANDING* 77
    I.   The Structure of Standing Doctrine 77
        California v. Texas 77
        Uzuegbunam v. Preczewski 79
    II. Congressional Power to Create Standing 80
        TransUnion LLC v. Ramirez 80
3. *TIMING OF ADJUDICATION* 82
    I.   Mootness 82

TABLE OF CASES

The principal cases are in bold type.

American Legion v. American Humanist Ass'n, 61
Americans for Prosperity Foundation v. Bonta, 47, 58, 60
Apodaca v. Oregon, 32
Arthrex, Inc., United States v., 18
Barr v. American Association of Political Consultants, Inc., 45
Benisek v. Lamone, 8
Berisha v. Lawson, 44
Bostock v. Clayton County, 71
Bowen v. Roy, 67
Bucklew v. Precythe, 42
Burr, United States v., 20
Bush v. Vera, 3
California v. Texas, 13, 77
Cedar Point Nursery v. Hasid, 29
Collins v. Yellen, 18
Common Cause v. Rucho, 8
DaimlerChrysler Corp. v. Cuno, 2
Davis v. Bandemer, 3, 72
Department of Homeland Security v. Regents of University of California, 71
Department of Homeland Security v. Thuraissigiam, 11
Dobbs v. Jackson Women's Health, 34
Doe v. Reed, 59
Espinoza v. Montana Department of Revenue, 63
Ford v. Wainwright, 41
Fulton v. City of Philadelphia, 66
Gill v. Whitford, 10
Gundy v. United States, 15
Hallock, Helvering v., 37
Hunt v. Cromartie, 3
Iancu v. Brunetti, 45
Jacobson v. Massachusetts, 33
Jones v. Missisippi, 41
June Medical Services L. L. C. v. Russo, 35, 79
League of United Latin American Citizens v. Perry, 3
Little Sisters of the Poor Saints Peter and Paul Home v. Pennsylvania, 62
Madison v. Alabama, 41
Mahanoy Area School District v. B. L., 48
Manhattan Community Access Corp. v. Halleck, 75
McKee v. Cosby, 44

Mt. Healthy City Bd. of Educ. v. Doyle, 44
Murphy v. National Collegiate Athletic Association, 46
National Federation of Independent Business v. Sebelius, 77
New York State Rifle & Pistol Ass'n v. City of New York, 40, 82
New York State Rifle v. Corlett, 41
Nieves v. Bartlett, 43
Our Lady of Guadalupe School v. Morrissey-Berru, 65
Payne v. Tennessee, 37
Perkins, United States v., 16
Ramos v. Louisiana, 32
Rucho v. Common Cause, 1
Seila Law LLC v. Consumer Financial Protection Bureau, 16, 78
Senate Select Committee on Presidential Campaign Activities v. Nixon, 23
Shaw v. Reno, 2
Shelton v. Tucker, 58
Sherbert v. Verner, 67
South Bay Pentecostal Church v. Newsom, 68
Tandon v. Newsom, 68
Tennessee Wine and Spirits Retailers Ass'n v. Tennessee Alcoholic Beverage Comm'n, 27
Timbs v. Indiana, 31
TransUnion LLC v. Ramirez, 80
Trump v. Mazars USA, LLP, 22
Trump v. Vance, 19
Uzuegbunam v. Preczewski, 79, 82
Vasquez v. Hillery, 37
Vieth v. Jubelirer, 3, 72
Wesberry v. Sanders, 2

TABLE OF AUTHORITIES

---

1 W. Blackstone, *Commentaries on the Laws of England* 69 (1765), 36

2 *Records of the Federal Convention of 1787*, p. 430 (M. Farrand ed. 1966), 2

3 Edmund Burke, *Reflections on the Revolution in France* 110 (1790), 37

Black's Law Dictionary 1696 (11th ed. 2019), 36

Dorf, Michael C., *Challengers to the Affordable Care Act Lose their Third Supreme Court Case: Will They Bring a Fourth?*, VERDICT (June 22, 2021), 13

Fallon, Richard H., Jr., *Facial Challenges, Saving Constructions, and Statutory Severability*, 99 Tex.L.Rev. 215 (2020), 79

Jackson, Robert, *Decisional Law and Stare Decisis*, 30 A.B.A.J. 334 (1944), 37

Logan, David, *Rescuing Our Democracy by Rethinking* New York Times v. Sullivan, 81 Ohio St. L.J. 759 (2020), 44

Scalia, Antonin, *The Rule of Law as a Law of Rules*, 56 U.Chi.L.Rev. 1175 (1989), 38

Sunstein, Cass R., *Falsehoods and the First Amendment*, 33 Harv. J.L. & Tech. 388 (2020), 44

The Federalist No. 47 (J. Madison), 17

The Federalist No. 78, p. 529 (J. Cooke ed. 1961) (A. Hamilton), 37

2021 SUPPLEMENT TO

CONSTITUTIONAL LAW

CASES, COMMENTS, AND QUESTIONS

Thirteenth Edition

CHAPTER 1

NATURE AND SCOPE OF JUDICIAL REVIEW

■ ■ ■

2. POLITICAL QUESTIONS

P. 41, after *Nixon v. United States*:

RUCHO V. COMMON CAUSE
588 U.S. ___, 139 S.Ct. 2484, 204 L.Ed.2d 931 (2019).

CHIEF JUSTICE ROBERTS delivered the opinion of the Court.

Voters and other plaintiffs in North Carolina and Maryland challenged their States' congressional districting maps as unconstitutional partisan gerrymanders. The North Carolina plaintiffs complained that the State's districting plan discriminated against Democrats; the Maryland plaintiffs complained that their State's plan discriminated against Republicans. The plaintiffs alleged that the gerrymandering violated the First Amendment, the Equal Protection Clause of the Fourteenth Amendment, the Elections Clause, and Article I, § 2, of the Constitution.

[All agree that the partisan gerrymanders at issue in the two cases were deliberate and at least initially highly effective. In *Rucho*, the North Carolina case] one of the two Republicans chairing the redistricting committee [explained] that the map was drawn with the aim of electing ten Republicans and three Democrats because he did "not believe it [would be] possible to draw a map with 11 Republicans and 2 Democrats." One Democratic state senator objected that entrenching the 10–3 advantage for Republicans was not "fair, reasonable, [or] balanced" because, as recently as 2012, "Democratic congressional candidates had received more votes on a statewide basis than Republican candidates." [In] November 2016, North Carolina conducted congressional elections using the 2016 Plan [at issue in the litigation], and Republican candidates won 10 of the 13 congressional districts.

[The] second case before us is *Lamone v. Benisek*. In 2011, the Maryland Legislature—dominated by Democrats—undertook to redraw the lines of that State's eight congressional districts. The Governor at the time, Democrat Martin O'Malley, [appointed] a redistricting committee to help redraw the map. [The] Governor later testified that his aim was to "use the redistricting process to change the overall composition of

Maryland's congressional delegation to 7 Democrats and 1 Republican by flipping" one district. [The] 2011 Plan accomplished that by moving roughly 360,000 voters out of the Sixth District and moving 350,000 new voters in. Overall, the Plan reduced the number of registered Republicans in the Sixth District by about 66,000 and increased the number of registered Democrats by about 24,000. The map was adopted by a party-line vote. It was used in the 2012 election and succeeded in flipping the Sixth District. A Democrat has held the seat ever since.

[In] these cases we are asked to decide an important question of constitutional law. "But before we do so, we must find that the question is presented in a 'case' or 'controversy' that is, in James Madison's words, 'of a Judiciary Nature.'" *DaimlerChrysler Corp. v. Cuno*, 547 U.S. 332, 342 (2006) (quoting 2 Records of the Federal Convention of 1787, p. 430 (M. Farrand ed. 1966)). [The] question here is whether there is an "appropriate role for the Federal Judiciary" in remedying the problem of partisan gerrymandering—whether such claims are claims of *legal* right, resolvable according to *legal* principles, or political questions that must find their resolution elsewhere.

Partisan gerrymandering is nothing new. Nor is frustration with it. [The] Framers addressed the election of Representatives to Congress in the Elections Clause. Art. I, § 4, cl. 1. That provision assigns to state legislatures the power to prescribe the "Times, Places and Manner of holding Elections" for Members of Congress, while giving Congress the power to "make or alter" any such regulations. [The Court here cited historical examples of congressional regulation before recognizing that only a requirement that states use single-member districts remains in place today.]

[Appellants] suggest that, through the Elections Clause, the Framers set aside electoral issues such as the one before us as questions that only Congress can resolve. We do not agree. In two areas—one-person, one-vote and racial gerrymandering—our cases have held that there is a role for the courts with respect to at least some issues that could arise from a State's drawing of congressional districts. See *Wesberry v. Sanders*, 376 U.S. 1 (1964); *Shaw v. Reno*, 509 U.S. 630 (1993).

But the history is not irrelevant. The Framers were aware of electoral districting problems and considered what to do about them. [At] no point was there a suggestion that the federal courts had a role to play. Nor was there any indication that the Framers had ever heard of courts doing such a thing.

[Partisan] gerrymandering claims have proved far more difficult to adjudicate [than one-person, one-vote cases and cases involving racial discrimination]. The basic reason is that, while it is illegal for a jurisdiction to depart from the one-person, one-vote rule, or to engage in racial discrimination in districting, "a jurisdiction may engage in constitutional political gerrymandering." *Hunt v. Cromartie*, 526 U.S. 541, 551 (1999) (citing *Bush v. Vera*, 517 U.S. 952, 968 (1996)).

To hold that legislators cannot take partisan interests into account when drawing district lines would essentially countermand the Framers' decision to entrust districting to political entities. The "central problem" is not determining whether a jurisdiction has engaged in partisan gerrymandering. It is "determining when political gerrymandering has gone too far." *Vieth* [*v. Jubelirer*, 541 U.S. 267, 296 (2004) (plurality opinion). The Court here recounted its prior confrontations will challenges to political gerrymandering. In *Davis v. Bandemer*, 478 U.S. 109 (1986)), a majority thought the case was justiciable but splintered over the proper standard to apply. Four Justices (White, Brennan, Marshall, and Blackmun, JJ.) would have required proof of "intentional discrimination against an identifiable political group and an actual discriminatory effect on that group." Two Justices (Powell and Stevens, JJ.) would have focused on "whether the boundaries of the voting districts have been distorted deliberately and arbitrarily to achieve illegitimate ends." But O'Connor, J., joined by Burger, C.J., and Rehnquist, J., would have held that partisan gerrymandering claims pose political questions because the Equal Protection Clause simply "does not supply judicially manageable standards for resolving" them.]

[Eighteen years later, in *Vieth*, Justice Scalia's plurality opinion also would have held challenges to gerrymanders nonjusticiable due to an absence of judicially manageable standards.] Kennedy, J., concurring in the judgment, noted "the lack of comprehensive and neutral principles for drawing electoral boundaries [and] the absence of rules to limit and confine judicial intervention." He nonetheless left open the possibility that "in another case a standard might emerge." Four Justices dissented.

[The] question [in appraising political gerrymandering claims] is one of degree: How to "provid[e] a standard for deciding how much partisan dominance is too much." *League of United Latin American Citizens v. Perry*, 548 U.S. 399, 420 (2006) (opinion of Kennedy, J.). And it is vital in such circumstances that the Court act only in accord with especially clear standards: "With uncertain limits, intervening courts—even when proceeding with best intentions—would risk assuming political, not legal, responsibility for a process that often produces ill will and distrust." *Vieth*, 541 U.S., at 307 (opinion of Kennedy, J.).

[Partisan] gerrymandering claims invariably sound in a desire for proportional representation. * * * "Our cases, however, clearly foreclose any claim that the Constitution requires proportional representation." [Unable] to claim that the Constitution requires proportional representation outright, plaintiffs inevitably ask the courts to make their own political judgment about how much representation particular political parties *deserve*—based on the votes of their supporters—and to rearrange the challenged districts to achieve that end. But federal courts are not equipped to apportion political power as a matter of fairness, nor is there any basis for concluding that they were authorized to do so.

[The] initial difficulty in settling on a "clear, manageable and politically neutral" test for fairness is that it is not even clear what fairness looks like in this context. [Fairness] may mean a greater number of competitive districts. [On] the other hand, perhaps the ultimate objective of a "fairer" share of seats in the congressional delegation is most readily achieved by yielding to the gravitational pull of proportionality and engaging in cracking and packing, to ensure each party its "appropriate" share of "safe" seats. [Or] perhaps fairness should be measured by adherence to "traditional" districting criteria, such as maintaining political subdivisions, keeping communities of interest together, and protecting incumbents.

[Deciding] among just these different visions of fairness (you can imagine many others) poses basic questions that are political, not legal. There are no legal standards discernible in the Constitution for making such judgments, let alone limited and precise standards that are clear, manageable, and politically neutral.

[Even] assuming the court knew which version of fairness to be looking for, there are no discernible and manageable standards for deciding whether there has been a violation. [Appellees] contend that if we can adjudicate one-person, one-vote claims, we can also assess partisan gerrymandering claims. [But] "vote dilution" in the one-person, one-vote cases refers to the idea that each vote must carry equal weight. [That] requirement does not extend to political parties. It does not mean that each party must be influential in proportion to its number of supporters.

Appellees and the dissent propose a number of "tests" for evaluating partisan gerrymandering claims, but none meets the need for a limited and precise standard that is judicially discernible and manageable. And none provides a solid grounding for judges to take the extraordinary step of reallocating power and influence between political parties.

[The District Court in the North Carolina case used a test that involved a "predominant" legislative purpose coupled with a demand for] a showing "that the dilution of the votes of supporters of a disfavored party in a particular district [is] likely to persist in subsequent elections such that an elected representative from the favored party in the district will not feel a need to be responsive to constituents who support the disfavored party."

[The] District Court's "predominant intent" prong is borrowed from the racial gerrymandering context. [If] district lines were drawn for the purpose of separating racial groups, then they are subject to strict scrutiny because "race-based decisionmaking is inherently suspect." But determining that lines were drawn on the basis of partisanship does not indicate that the districting was improper. A permissible intent—securing partisan advantage—does not become constitutionally impermissible, like racial discrimination, when that permissible intent "predominates."

The District Court tried to limit the reach of its test by requiring plaintiffs to show, in addition to predominant partisan intent, that vote dilution "is likely to persist" to such a degree that the elected representative will feel free to ignore the concerns of the supporters of the minority party. But "[t]o allow district courts to strike down apportionment plans on the basis of their prognostications as to the outcome of future elections . . . invites 'findings' on matters as to which neither judges nor anyone else can have any confidence." *Bandemer*, 478 U.S., at 160 (opinion of O'Connor, J.).

[The] District Courts also found partisan gerrymandering claims justiciable under the First Amendment, coalescing around a basic three-part test: proof of intent to burden individuals based on their voting history or party affiliation; an actual burden on political speech or associational rights; and a causal link between the invidious intent and actual burden. [To] begin, there are no restrictions on speech, association, or any other First Amendment activities in the districting plans at issue. [The] plaintiffs' argument is that partisanship in districting should be regarded as simple discrimination against supporters of the opposing party on the basis of political viewpoint. [It] provides no standard for determining when partisan activity goes too far.

As for actual burden, the slight anecdotal evidence found sufficient by the District Courts in these cases shows that this too is not a serious standard for separating constitutional from unconstitutional partisan gerrymandering. [How] much of a decline in voter engagement is enough to constitute a First Amendment burden? How many door knocks must go unanswered? How many petitions unsigned? How many calls for volunteers unheeded

The dissent proposes using a State's own districting criteria as a neutral baseline from which to measure how extreme a partisan gerrymander is. The dissent would have us line up all the possible maps drawn using those criteria according to the partisan distribution they would produce. Distance from the "median" map would indicate whether a particular districting plan harms supporters of one party to an unconstitutional extent.

As an initial matter, it does not make sense to use criteria that will vary from State to State and year to year as the baseline for determining whether a gerrymander violates the Federal Constitution. The degree of partisan advantage that the Constitution tolerates should not turn on criteria offered by the gerrymanderers themselves.

[Even] if we were to accept the dissent's proposed baseline, it would return us to "the original unanswerable question (How much political motivation and effect is too much?)." *Vieth*, 541 U.S., at 296–297 (plurality opinion). Would twenty percent away from the median map be okay? Forty percent? Sixty percent? Why or why not?

[The] dissent argues that there are other instances in law where matters of degree are left to the courts. True enough. But those instances typically involve constitutional or statutory provisions or common law confining and guiding the exercise of judicial discretion. [Here], on the other hand, the Constitution provides no basis whatever to guide the exercise of judicial discretion. [The] only provision in the Constitution that specifically addresses the matter assigns it to the political branches. See Art. I, § 4, cl. 1. [The Court next dismissed arguments based on the Elections Clause and Article I, § 2.]

Excessive partisanship in districting leads to results that reasonably seem unjust. But the fact that such gerrymandering is "incompatible with democratic principles," does not mean that the solution lies with the federal judiciary. [Federal] judges have no license to reallocate political power between the two major political parties, with no plausible grant of authority in the Constitution, and no legal standards to limit and direct their decisions.

[Our] conclusion does not condone excessive partisan gerrymandering. Nor does our conclusion condemn complaints about districting to echo into a void. The States, for example, are actively addressing the issue on a number of fronts. [The Court here described state legislation, state ballot initiatives, and state constitutional amendments to limit partisan gerrymandering.]

[As] noted, the Framers gave Congress the power to do something about partisan gerrymandering in the Elections Clause. [The Court here described several bills introduced in Congress.] We express no view on any of these pending proposals. We simply note that the avenue for reform established by the Framers, and used by Congress in the past, remains open.

* * *

JUSTICE KAGAN, with whom JUSTICES GINSBURG, BREYER, and SOTOMAYOR join, dissenting.

For the first time ever, this Court refuses to remedy a constitutional violation because it thinks the task beyond judicial capabilities. [The] partisan gerrymanders in these cases deprived citizens of the most fundamental of their constitutional rights: the rights to participate equally in the political process, to join with others to advance political beliefs, and to choose their political representatives. [If] left unchecked, gerrymanders like the ones here may irreparably damage our system of government. And checking them is *not* beyond the courts. The majority's abdication comes just when courts across the country, including those below, have coalesced around manageable judicial standards to resolve partisan gerrymandering claims.

[The] majority concedes (really, how could it not?) that gerrymandering is "incompatible with democratic principles." [That] recognition would seem to demand a response. The majority offers two ideas * * *. One is that the political process can deal with the problem—a proposition so dubious on its face that I feel secure in delaying my answer for some time. The other is that political gerrymanders have always been with us. To its credit, the majority does not frame that point as an originalist constitutional argument. After all (as the majority rightly notes), racial and residential gerrymanders were also once with us, but the Court has done something about that fact. The majority's idea instead seems to be that if we have lived with partisan gerrymanders so long, we will survive.

That complacency has no cause. [While] bygone mapmakers may have drafted three or four alternative districting plans, today's mapmakers can generate thousands of possibilities at the touch of a key—and then choose the one giving their party maximum advantage (usually while still meeting traditional districting requirements). The effect is to make gerrymanders far more effective and durable than before, insulating politicians against all but the most titanic shifts in the political tides.

[Partisan] gerrymandering of the kind before us not only subverts democracy (as if that weren't bad enough). It violates individuals' constitutional rights as well. [That] practice implicates the Fourteenth Amendment's Equal Protection Clause. [And] partisan gerrymandering implicates the First Amendment too. That Amendment gives its greatest protection to political beliefs, speech, and association. Yet partisan gerrymanders subject certain voters to "disfavored treatment"—again, counting their votes for less—precisely because of "their voting history [and] their expression of political views." *Vieth*, 541 U.S., at 314 (opinion of Kennedy, J.).

[The] majority never disagrees; it appears to accept the "principle that each person must have an equal say in the election of representatives." And indeed, without this settled and shared understanding that cases like these inflict constitutional injury, the question of whether there are judicially manageable standards for resolving them would never come up.

So the only way to understand the majority's opinion is as follows: In the face of grievous harm to democratic governance and flagrant infringements on individuals' rights—in the face of escalating partisan manipulation whose compatibility with this Nation's values and law no one defends—the majority declines to provide any remedy. [I'll] give the majority this one—and important—thing: It identifies some dangers everyone should want to avoid. Judges should not be apportioning political power based on their own vision of electoral fairness, whether proportional representation or any other. And judges should not be striking down maps left, right, and center, on the view that every smidgen of politics is a smidgen too much. Respect for state legislative processes—and restraint in the exercise of judicial authority—counsels intervention in only egregious cases.

But in throwing up its hands, the majority misses something under its nose: What it says can't be done *has* been done. Over the past several years, federal courts across the country—including, but not exclusively, in the decisions below—have largely converged on a standard for adjudicating partisan gerrymandering claims (striking down both Democratic and Republican districting plans in the process).

[Start] with the standard the lower courts used. [B]oth courts (like others around the country) used basically the same three-part test to decide whether the plaintiffs had made out a vote dilution claim. As many legal standards do, that test has three parts: (1) intent; (2) effects; and (3) causation. First, the plaintiffs challenging a districting plan must prove that state officials' "predominant purpose" in drawing a district's lines was to "entrench [their party] in power" by diluting the votes of citizens favoring its rival. [Justice Kagan here cited *Common Cause v. Rucho*, 318 F. Supp. 3d 777, 805–806 (M.D.N.C. 2018).] Second, the plaintiffs must establish that the lines drawn in fact have the intended effect by "substantially" diluting their votes. [Justice Kagan here cited *Benisek v. Lamone*, 348 F. Supp. 3d 493, 498 (Md. 2018).] And third, if the plaintiffs make those showings, the State must come up with a legitimate, non-partisan justification to save its map. If you are a lawyer, you know that this test looks utterly ordinary. It is the sort of thing courts work with every day.

[The] majority's response to the District Courts' purpose analysis is discomfiting. The majority does not contest the lower courts' findings; how could it? Instead, the majority says that state officials' intent to entrench their party in power is perfectly "permissible," even when it is the predominant factor in drawing district lines. But that is wrong. [W]hen political actors have a specific and predominant intent to entrench themselves in power by manipulating district lines, that goes too far.

[On] to the second step of the analysis, where the plaintiffs must prove that the districting plan substantially dilutes their votes. [Consider] the sort of evidence used in North Carolina first. There, the plaintiffs demonstrated the districting plan's effects mostly by relying on what might be called the "extreme outlier approach." [The] approach—which also has recently been used in Michigan and Ohio litigation—begins by using advanced computing technology to randomly generate a large collection of districting plans that incorporate the State's physical and political geography and meet its declared districting criteria, *except for* partisan gain. [The] further out on the tail, the more extreme the partisan distortion and the more significant the vote dilution.

Using that approach, the North Carolina plaintiffs offered a boatload of alternative districting plans—all showing that the State's map was an out-out-out-outlier. One expert produced 3,000 maps, adhering in the way described above to the districting criteria that the North Carolina redistricting committee had used, other than partisan advantage. To calculate the partisan outcome of those maps, the expert also used the same election data (a composite of seven elections) that [a North Carolina expert] had employed when devising the North Carolina plan in the first instance. [Every] single one of the 3,000 maps would have produced at least one more Democratic House Member than the State's actual map, and 77% would have elected three or four more. [Based] on those and other findings, the District Court determined that the North Carolina plan substantially dilutes the plaintiffs' votes.

Because the Maryland gerrymander involved just one district, the evidence in that case was far simpler—but no less powerful for that. [In] the old Sixth [District], 47% of registered voters were Republicans and only 36% Democrats. But in the new Sixth, 44% of registered voters were Democrats and only 33% Republicans. That reversal of the district's partisan composition translated into four consecutive Democratic victories, including in a wave election year for Republicans (2014). In what was once a party stronghold, Republicans now have little or no chance to elect their preferred candidate. The District Court thus found that the gerrymandered Maryland map substantially dilutes Republicans' votes.

[By] substantially diluting the votes of citizens favoring their rivals, the politicians of one party had succeeded in entrenching themselves in office. They had beat democracy.

The majority's broadest claim, as I've noted, is that this is a price we must pay because judicial oversight of partisan gerrymandering cannot be "politically neutral" or "manageable." [Consider] neutrality first. Contrary to the majority's suggestion, the District Courts did not have to—and in fact did not—choose among competing visions of electoral fairness. That is because they did not try to compare the State's actual map to an "ideally fair" one (whether based on proportional representation or some other criterion). Instead, they looked at the difference between what the State did and what the State would have done if politicians hadn't been intent on partisan gain. Or put differently, the comparator (or baseline or touchstone) is the result not of a judge's philosophizing but of the State's own characteristics and judgments.

[The] majority's sole response misses the point. According to the majority, "it does not make sense to use" a State's own (non-partisan) districting criteria as the baseline from which to measure partisan gerrymandering because those criteria "will vary from State to State and year to year." But that is a virtue, not a vice—a feature, not a bug.

[The] majority's "how much is too much" critique fares no better than its neutrality argument. How about the following for a first-cut answer: This much is too much. By any measure, a map that produces a greater partisan skew than any of 3,000 randomly generated maps (all with the State's political geography and districting criteria built in) reflects "too much" partisanship. Think about what I just said: The absolute worst of 3,001 possible maps. The *only one* that could produce a 10–3 partisan split even as Republicans got a bare majority of the statewide vote. And again: How much is too much? This much is too much: A map that without any evident non-partisan districting reason (to the contrary) shifted the composition of a district from 47% Republicans and 36% Democrats to 33% Republicans and 42% Democrats. A map that in 2011 was responsible for the largest partisan swing of a congressional district in the country.

And if the majority thought that approach too case-specific, it could have used the lower courts' general standard—focusing on "predominant" purpose and "substantial" effects—without fear of indeterminacy. I do not take even the majority to claim that courts are incapable of investigating whether legislators mainly intended to seek partisan advantage.

[Nor] is there any reason to doubt, as the majority does, the competence of courts to determine whether a district map "substantially" dilutes the votes of a rival party's supporters from the everything-but-partisanship baseline described above. [As] this Court recently noted, "the law is full of instances" where a judge's decision rests on "estimating rightly ... some matter of degree"—including the "substantial[ity]" of risk or harm.

[This] Court has long understood that it has a special responsibility to remedy violations of constitutional rights resulting from politicians' districting decisions. [The] need for judicial review is at its most urgent in cases like these. "For here, politicians' incentives conflict with voters' interests, leaving citizens without any political remedy for their constitutional harms." [*Gill v. Whitford*, 138 S.Ct. 1916, 1941 (2018),] (Kagan, J., concurring). Those harms arise because politicians want to stay in office. No one can look to them for effective relief.

[Here Kagan, J., argued that Congress and state political processes were unlikely to provide an effective remedy After noting that the majority had also recognized state courts as a possible source of relief—since the political question doctrine does not apply to them—she asked:] But what do those courts know that this Court does not? If they can develop and apply neutral and manageable standards to identify unconstitutional gerrymanders, why couldn't we?

[The] practices challenged in these cases imperil our system of government. Part of the Court's role in that system is to defend its foundations. None is more important than free and fair elections. With respect but deep sadness, I dissent.

P. 44, substitute for note 3:

The topic of "judicially manageable standards" is extensively discussed and debated in *Rucho v. Common Cause*, which appears immediately above in this Supplement.

3. CONGRESSIONAL REGULATION OF JUDICIAL POWER

P. 60, at the end of note 9:

Department of Homeland Security v. Thuraissigiam, 140 S.Ct. 1959 (2020), found that a statute precluding habeas corpus review did not violate the Suspension Clause as applied to a noncitizen, apprehended within twenty-five yards of his initial crossing of the U.S. border, who sought to challenge administrative determinations that he had failed to establish a "credible fear of persecution" if returned to his homeland. Alito, J.'s, opinion for the Court reasoned that because the petitioner did not seek a "traditional" release from custody—but rather a "new opportunity to apply for asylum," during the pendency of which since he would have remained in detention—he fell outside the scope of the writ as it existed when the Constitution was adopted. The Court also held that the denial of judicial review did not violate the Due Process Clause in the case of an alien who had neither lawfully entered the United States nor established significant contacts here. Breyer, J., joined by Ginsburg, J., concurred on the narrower ground that even if the petitioner would have had a right to habeas review of some issues bearing on the legality of his detention under the immigration laws, that right would not extend to claims as fact-bound as his. Sotomayor, J., joined by Kagan, J., dissented, affirming that the Suspension Clause entitled the petitioner to review of his claim that administrative officials had applied the wrong legal standard to his case.

CHAPTER 2

NATIONAL LEGISLATIVE POWER

■ ■ ■

3. THE NATIONAL TAXING AND SPENDING POWERS

I. REGULATION THROUGH TAXING

P. 143, at the end of note 1:

These questions were presented in CALIFORNIA v. TEXAS, 141 S.Ct. 2104 (2021), but the Court, in an opinion by BREYER, J., did not decide them on the ground that the plaintiffs lacked standing.

ALITO, J., joined by Gorsuch, J. dissented and would have reached the merits to find that zeroing out the tax rendered the mandate unconstitutional: "Congress cannot supplement its powers through the two-step process of passing a tax and then removing the tax but leaving in place a provision that is otherwise beyond its enumerated powers."

Is that the best characterization of what Congress did? Consider Michael C. Dorf, *Challengers to the Affordable Care Act Lose their Third Supreme Court Case: Will They Bring a Fourth?*, VERDICT (June 22, 2021), verdict.justia.com/ 2021/06/22/challengers-to-the-affordable-care-act-lose-their-third-supreme-court-case: "The post-2017 version of the ACA gives people a choice: buy health insurance [or] don't if you don't want to. [And] Congress undoubtedly has the power to instruct people that they don't have to do anything."

CHAPTER 3

DISTRIBUTION OF FEDERAL POWERS: SEPARATION OF POWERS

■ ■ ■

2. CONGRESSIONAL ACTION AFFECTING "PRESIDENTIAL" POWERS

I. DELEGATION OF RULEMAKING POWER

P. 221, before note 2:

(e) *Future of the "intelligible principle" test.* Congress enacted the Sex Offender Registration and Notification Act (SORNA), in order to provide for greater uniformity among state sex-offender registration systems, delegating to the Attorney General "the authority to specify the applicability of [its] requirements" to "offenders convicted before the enactment of" SORNA. In GUNDY v. UNITED STATES, 139 S.Ct. 2116 (2019), the Court rejected a nondelegation challenge to SORNA. KAGAN, J., announced the judgment of the Court and authored an opinion joined by three colleagues rejecting petitioner's contention that the Act "grants the Attorney General plenary power to determine SORNA's applicability to pre-Act offenders. [If] that were so, we would face a nondelegation question. But [the] Attorney General's discretion extends only to considering and addressing feasibility issues," thus satisfying the intelligible principle requirement.

Concurring only in the judgment, ALITO, J., agreed with that conclusion, adding that he would be willing to reconsider the post-*Schechter* nondelegation case law if a majority of the Court were to do so. GORSUCH, J., joined by Roberts, C.J., and Thomas, J., did not wish to wait. He dissented and would have reformed the doctrine by relying on a test that focuses on three questions: "Does the statute assign to the executive only the responsibility to make factual findings? Does it set forth the facts that the executive must consider and the criteria against which to measure them? And most importantly, did Congress, and not the Executive Branch, make the policy judgments? Only then can we fairly say that a statute contains the kind of intelligible principle the Constitution demands." KAVANAUGH, J., did not participate in *Gundy*.

III. APPOINTMENT AND REMOVAL OF OFFICERS

P. 254, before note 5:

(d) SEILA LAW LLC v. CONSUMER FINANCIAL PROTECTION BUREAU, 140 S.Ct. 2183 (2020), concerned a restriction on the President's power to remove the Director of the Consumer Financial Protection Bureau (CFPB) prior to the expiration of a five-year term. The Supreme Court, per ROBERTS, C.J., held the restriction unconstitutional:

"In the wake of the 2008 financial crisis, Congress [through the Dodd-Frank Act] established the [CFPB], an independent regulatory agency tasked with ensuring that consumer debt products are safe and transparent. In organizing the CFPB, Congress deviated from the structure of nearly every other independent administrative agency in our history. Instead of placing the agency under the leadership of a board with multiple members, Congress provided that the CFPB would be led by a single Director, who serves for a longer term than the President and cannot be removed by the President except for inefficiency, neglect, or malfeasance. The CFPB Director has no boss, peers, or voters to report to. Yet the Director wields vast rulemaking, enforcement, and adjudicatory authority over a significant portion of the U.S. economy. The question before us is whether this arrangement violates the Constitution's separation of powers.

"Our precedents have recognized only two exceptions to the President's unrestricted removal power. In *Humphrey's Executor* we held that Congress could create expert agencies led by a *group* of principal officers removable by the President only for good cause. And in *United States v. Perkins*, 116 U.S. 483 (1886) [which upheld tenure protections for a naval cadet-engineer], and *Morrison* we held that Congress could provide tenure protections to certain *inferior* officers with narrowly defined duties.

"We are now asked to extend these precedents to a new configuration: an independent agency that wields significant executive power and is run by a single individual who cannot be removed by the President unless certain statutory criteria are met. We decline to take that step. While we need not and do not revisit our prior decisions allowing certain limitations on the President's removal power, there are compelling reasons not to extend those precedents to the novel context of an independent agency led by a single Director. Such an agency lacks a foundation in historical practice and clashes with constitutional structure by concentrating power in a unilateral actor insulated from Presidential control."

The Court nonetheless denied relief to the petitioner, a California-based law firm that provided debt-related legal services to clients and that resisted a subpoena from the CFPB on the ground that, in light of the unconstitutional tenure protection for the Director, the agency had no lawful authority. In a portion of his lead opinion joined only by Alito and Kavanaugh, JJ., the Chief Justice rejected petitioner's plea: "The provisions of the Dodd-Frank Act bearing on the CFPB's structure and duties remain fully operative without the offending tenure restriction. Those provisions are capable of functioning independently, and there is nothing in the text or history of the Dodd-Frank Act that demonstrates Congress would have preferred *no* CFPB to a CFPB supervised by the President. Quite the opposite. [The] Dodd-Frank Act contains an express severability clause." Because the Justices who dissented on the merits concurred in the judgment with respect to severability, the petitioner was denied relief but the CFPB Director was rendered subject to removal at will by the President.

THOMAS, J., joined by Gorsuch, J., concurred in the merits: "*Humphrey's Executor* does not comport with the Constitution. [The] Constitution does not permit the creation of officers exercising 'quasi-legislative' and 'quasi-judicial powers' in 'quasi-legislative' and 'quasi-judicial agencies.' No such powers or agencies exist. Congress lacks the authority to delegate its legislative power, and it cannot authorize the use of judicial power by officers acting outside of the bounds of Article III. Nor can Congress create agencies that straddle multiple branches of Government. The Constitution sets out three branches of Government and provides each with a different form of power—legislative, executive, and judicial. [If] any remnant of *Humphrey's Executor* is still standing, it certainly is not enough to justify the numerous, unaccountable independent agencies that currently exercise vast executive power outside the bounds of our constitutional structure."

With respect to the remedy, THOMAS, J., joined by Gorsuch, J., dissented: "The Federal Judiciary does not have the power to excise, erase, alter, or otherwise strike down a statute. And the Court's reference to severability as a 'remedy' is inaccurate. Traditional remedies—like injunctions, declarations, or damages—operate with respect to specific parties, not on legal rules in the abstract [citations and internal quotation marks omitted]."

KAGAN, J., joined by Ginsburg, Breyer, and Sotomayor, JJ., concluded that "*if* the agency's removal provision is unconstitutional, it should be severed," but dissented on the merits: "The majority offers the civics class version of separation of powers—call it the Schoolhouse Rock definition of the phrase. [Yet,] as James Madison stated, the creation of distinct branches 'did not mean that these departments ought to have no partial agency in, or no controul over the acts of each other.' The Federalist No. 47. [The] founding era closed without any agreement that Congress lacked the power to curb the President's removal authority. And as it kept that question open, Congress took the first steps— which would launch a tradition—of distinguishing financial regulators from diplomatic and military officers. The latter mainly helped the President carry out his own constitutional duties in foreign relations and war. The former chiefly carried out statutory duties, fulfilling functions Congress had assigned to their offices. In addressing the new Nation's finances, Congress had begun to use its powers under the Necessary and Proper Clause to design effective administrative institutions. And that included taking steps to insulate certain officers from political influence. As the decades and centuries passed, those efforts picked up steam. Confronting new economic, technological, and social conditions, Congress—and often the President—saw new needs for pockets of independence within the federal bureaucracy. And that was especially so, again, when it came to financial regulation.

"[Congress's] choice to put a single director, rather than a multimember commission, at the CFPB's head violates no principle of separation of powers. [To] make sense on the majority's own terms, the distinction between singular and plural agency heads must rest on a theory about why the former more easily 'slip' from the President's grasp. But [the] opposite is more likely to be true: To the extent that such matters are measurable, individuals are easier than groups to supervise."

The Court relied on *Seila Law* in COLLINS v. YELLEN, 141 S.Ct. 1761 (2021), to invalidate the Federal Housing Finance Agency (FHFA), which is tasked by statute with supervising mortgage financing companies Fannie Mae and Freddie Mac. Congress placed the FHFA under a single Director removable by the President only "for cause." ALITO, J., spoke for the Court. Rejecting the contention that the FHFA's limited responsibilities relative to those of the CFPB distinguished *Seila Law*, he wrote that "the nature and breadth of an agency's authority is not dispositive in determining whether Congress may limit the President's power to remove its head. The President's removal power serves vital purposes even when the officer subject to removal is not the head of one of the largest and most powerful agencies."

SOTOMAYOR, J., joined by Breyer, J., dissented in part: "*Seila Law* did not hold that an independent agency may never be run by a single individual with tenure protection. Rather, that decision stated, repeatedly, that its holding was limited to a single-director agency with 'significant executive power.'"

Justices Thomas, Gorsuch, and Kagan joined in part by Breyer and Sotomayor, each wrote separately, concurring in whole or in part with the Court's remand for a determination of whether the removal restriction harmed the plaintiffs.

P. 257, after the carryover paragraph, insert the following:

UNITED STATES v. ARTHREX, INC., 141 S.Ct. 1970 (2021), per ROBERTS, C.J., was a successful challenge to the appointment of Administrative Patent Judges (APJs) responsible, among other things, for adjudicating the validity of previously issued patents when sitting in panels of the Patent Trial and Appeal Board. Although the Director of the Patent and Trademark Office, a principal officer, exercised significant control over APJs, who were appointed by the Secretary of Commerce and thus inferior officers, he lacked the ability to direct results: "Given the insulation of [their] decisions from any executive review, the President can neither oversee the [APJs] himself nor attribute [their] failings to those whom he *can* oversee. APJs accordingly exercise power that conflicts with the design of the Appointments Clause to preserve political accountability." (Citations and internal quotation marks omitted). In a portion of his opinion that spoke only for a plurality, the Chief Justice concluded that the proper remedy was to authorize the Director to review Board decisions, thus rendering APJs inferior officers. (To enable a coherent judgment, Breyer, J., who dissented from the substantive holding, joined the plurality's judgment with respect to the remedy.)

THOMAS, J., joined by Breyer, Sotomayor, and Kagan, JJ., dissented, pointing to various mechanisms by which the Director could exercise "functional power over" APJs. The Director sets APJ pay, "prescribes uniform procedural rules and formulates policies and procedures for Board proceedings, ... designate[s] and de-designate[s] Board decisions as precedential, [issues] binding policy directives that govern the Board." In addition, the Director "may release instructions that include exemplary applications of patent laws to fact patterns, which the Board can refer to when presented with factually similar cases. [He] may designate which of the 250-plus administrative patent judges hear certain cases and may remove administrative patent judges from their specific assignments without cause. [And] If the administrative patent judges (somehow) reach a result he does not like, the Director can add more members to the panel— including himself—and order the case reheard. [And if] the administrative patent judges (somehow) reach a result he does not like, the Director can add more members to the panel—including himself—and order the case reheard." (Citations and internal quotation marks omitted).

3. EXECUTIVE PRIVILEGE AND IMMUNITY

P. 267, replace (b) and (c) with the following:

(b) TRUMP v. VANCE, 140 S.Ct. 2412 (2020), addressed, in a criminal context, a question the Court specifically left open in *Clinton*: whether a sitting [*issue*] President enjoys any kind of immunity in actions in *state* court. A state prosecutor in New York City initiated a wide-ranging investigation and on behalf of a grand jury issued a subpoena *duces tecum* to an accounting firm seeking financial records of President Trump and his businesses beginning six years before and continuing into his presidency. The President argued that he enjoys absolute immunity from state criminal processes while in office. All nine members of the Court rejected the absolute immunity claim. *unanimous → [president does not enjoy absolute immunity]*

ROBERTS, C.J., wrote for the Court: "In our judicial system, 'the public has a right to every man's evidence.' Since the earliest days of the Republic, 'every man' has included the President of the United States. Beginning with Jefferson and carrying on through Clinton, Presidents have uniformly testified or produced documents in criminal proceedings when called upon by federal courts. This case involves—so far as we and the parties can tell—the first *state* criminal subpoena directed to a President. The President contends that the subpoena is unenforceable."

Chief Justice Roberts began by describing the long history of federal courts compelling, and of Presidents complying with, subpoenas, with special

"every man" → includes the sitting president.

focus on the treason trial of Aaron Burr, at which Chief Justice Marshall, riding circuit, presided. *See United States v. Burr*, 25 F.Cas. 30 (No. 14,692d) (CC Va. 1807). "Burr moved for a subpoena *duces tecum* directed at Jefferson. [The] prosecution opposed the request, arguing that a President could not be subjected to such a subpoena and that the [document Burr sought] might contain state secrets. [The] President, Marshall declared, does not 'stand exempt from the general provisions of the constitution.' [At] common law the 'single reservation' to the duty to testify in response to a subpoena was 'the case of the king,' whose 'dignity' was seen as 'incompatible' with appearing 'under the process of the court.' But, as Marshall explained, a king is born to power and can 'do no wrong.' The President, by contrast, is 'of the people' and subject to the law. According to Marshall, the sole argument for exempting the President from testimonial obligations was that his 'duties as chief magistrate demand his whole time for national objects.' But, in Marshall's assessment, those demands were 'not unremitting.' And should the President's duties preclude his attendance at a particular time and place, a court could work that out upon return of the subpoena. Marshall also rejected the prosecution's argument that the President was immune from a subpoena *duces tecum* because executive papers might contain state secrets. 'A subpoena duces tecum,' he said, 'may issue to any person to whom an ordinary subpoena may issue.' [In] the two centuries since the Burr trial, successive Presidents have accepted Marshall's ruling that the Chief Executive is subject to subpoena.

"[The President] argues that the Supremacy Clause gives a sitting President absolute immunity from state criminal subpoenas because compliance with those subpoenas would categorically impair a President's performance of his Article II functions. The Solicitor General, arguing on behalf of the United States, agrees with much of the President's reasoning but does not commit to his bottom line. Instead, the Solicitor General urges us to resolve this case by holding that a state grand jury subpoena for a sitting President's personal records must, at the very least, 'satisfy a heightened standard of need . . . .'

"[The President concedes] that state grand juries are free to investigate a sitting President with an eye toward charging him after the completion of his term. [His] objection therefore must be limited to the *additional* distraction caused by the subpoena itself. But that argument runs up against the 200 years of precedent establishing that Presidents, and their official communications, are subject to judicial process even when the President is under investigation.

"[The] President next claims that the stigma of being subpoenaed will undermine his leadership at home and abroad. Notably, the Solicitor General does not endorse this argument, perhaps because we have twice denied absolute immunity claims by Presidents in cases involving allegations of serious misconduct [citing Presidents Nixon and Clinton].

"[Finally,] the President and the Solicitor General [argue] that, while federal prosecutors are accountable to and removable by the President, the

* federal prosecutors are accountable to & removable by the president.

2,300 district attorneys in this country are responsive to local constituencies, local interests, and local prejudices. [While] we cannot ignore the possibility that state prosecutors may have political motivations, [state and federal law] protect against the predicted abuse. [Moreover, t]he Supremacy Clause prohibits state judges and prosecutors from interfering with a President's official duties. [Any] effort to manipulate a President's policy decisions or to retaliate against a President for official acts through issuance of a subpoena would thus be an unconstitutional attempt to influence a superior sovereign exempt from such obstacles. We generally assume that state courts and prosecutors will observe constitutional limitations. Failing that, federal law allows a President to challenge any allegedly unconstitutional influence in a federal forum, as the President has done here [citations and internal quotation marks omitted].

"[Thus,] we cannot conclude that absolute immunity is necessary or appropriate under Article II or the Supremacy Clause. Our dissenting colleagues agree. [On] that point the Court is unanimous."

unanimously agree that absolute immunity is not appropriate.

The Court next considered "whether a state grand jury subpoena seeking a President's private papers must satisfy a heightened need standard." It rejected such a standard "for three reasons. First, such a heightened standard would extend protection designed for official documents to the President's private papers. [Second,] heightened protection against state subpoenas is [not] necessary for the Executive to fulfill his Article II functions. [If] the state subpoena is not issued to manipulate, the documents themselves are not protected, and the Executive is not impaired, then nothing in Article II or the Supremacy Clause supports holding state subpoenas to a higher standard than their federal counterparts. Finally, in the absence of a need to protect the Executive, the public interest in fair and effective law enforcement cuts in favor of comprehensive access to evidence."

3 reasons why court rejects a heightened standard.

Having rejected the President's and Solicitor General's categorical arguments, the Court allowed the possibility of "subpoena-specific constitutional challenges" and accordingly remanded to the lower courts.

KAVANAUGH, J., joined by Gorsuch, J., concurred in the judgment. Agreeing with the Court's rejection of absolute immunity, he would have applied the "demonstrated, specific need" standard of *Nixon*, which he distinguished from the "heightened need" standard proposed by the Solicitor General: "The *Nixon* standard ensures that a prosecutor's interest in subpoenaed information is sufficiently important to justify an intrusion on the Article II interests of the Presidency [and] reduces the risk of subjecting a President to unwarranted burdens, because it provides that a prosecutor may obtain a President's information only in certain defined circumstances. Although the Court adopted the *Nixon* standard in a different Article II context—there, involving the confidentiality of official, privileged information—[there] are also important Article II (and Supremacy Clause) interests at stake here."

Concurrence argues for the "demonstrated, specific need" standard.

THOMAS, J., also wrote separately in what he styled a dissent, although he agreed with the Court that the President lacks "absolute immunity from *issuance* of the subpoena. But he may be entitled to relief against its *enforcement.* [The] majority recognizes that the President can seek relief from enforcement, but it does not vacate and remand for the lower courts to address this question. I would do so and instruct them to apply the standard articulated by Chief Justice Marshall in *Burr*: If the President is unable to comply because of his official duties, then he is entitled to injunctive and declaratory relief."

ALITO, J., also dissented, emphasizing that the President was effectively a target of the investigation. "In *McCulloch v. Maryland* [Ch. 2, Sec. 1], Maryland's sovereign taxing power had to yield, and in a similar way, a State's sovereign power to enforce its criminal laws must accommodate the indispensable role that the Constitution assigns to the Presidency. This must be the rule with respect to a state prosecution of a sitting President. Both the structure of the Government established by the Constitution and the Constitution's provisions on the impeachment and removal of a President make it clear that the prosecution of a sitting President is out of the question.

"If a sitting President were charged in New York County, would he be arrested and fingerprinted? He would presumably be required to appear for arraignment in criminal court, where the judge would set the conditions for his release. Could he be sent to Rikers Island or be required to post bail? Could the judge impose restrictions on his travel? If the President were scheduled to travel abroad—perhaps to attend a G-7 meeting—would he have to get judicial approval? [The] law applies equally to all persons, including a person who happens for a period of time to occupy the Presidency. But there is no question that the nature of the office demands in some instances that the application of laws be adjusted at least until the person's term in office ends.

"I agree with the Court that not all [subpoenas to the President] should be barred. There may be situations in which there is an urgent and critical need for the subpoenaed information. The situation in the Burr trial, where the documents at issue were sought by a criminal defendant to defend against a charge of treason, is a good example. But in a case like the one at hand, a subpoena should not be allowed unless a heightened standard is met."

(c) TRUMP v. MAZARS USA, LLP, 140 S.Ct. 2019 (2020), was decided the same day as *Trump v. Vance.* ROBERTS, C.J., again wrote for the Court: "[T]hree committees of the U.S. House of Representatives issued four subpoenas seeking information about the finances of President Donald J. Trump, his children, and affiliated businesses. We have held that the House has authority under the Constitution to issue subpoenas to assist it in carrying out its legislative responsibilities. The House asserts that the financial information sought here—encompassing a decade's worth of transactions by the President and his family—will help guide legislative reform in areas ranging from money laundering and terrorism to foreign involvement in U.S. elections. The President contends that the House lacked a valid legislative aim and instead sought these records to harass him, expose personal matters, and conduct law enforcement activities beyond its authority.

"[The] President's information is sought not by prosecutors or private parties in connection with a particular judicial proceeding, but by committees of Congress that have set forth broad legislative objectives. Congress and the President—the two political branches established by the Constitution—have an ongoing relationship that the Framers intended to feature both rivalry and reciprocity. [Historically], disputes over congressional demands for presidential documents have not ended up in court. Instead, they have been hashed out [politically]." Chief Justice Roberts then described negotiations and compromises reached between Congress and Presidents Washington, Jefferson, Reagan, and Clinton.

"Quoting *Nixon*, the President asserts that the House must establish a 'demonstrated, specific need' for the financial information, just as the Watergate special prosecutor was required to do in order to obtain the tapes. And drawing on *Senate Select Committee on Presidential Campaign Activities v. Nixon*, 498 F.2d 725 (1974)—the D.C. Circuit case refusing to enforce the Senate subpoena for the tapes—the President and the Solicitor General argue that the House must show that the financial information is 'demonstrably critical' to its legislative purpose. We disagree that these demanding standards apply here. Unlike the cases before us, *Nixon* and *Senate Select Committee* involved Oval Office communications over which the President asserted executive privilege. That privilege safeguards the public interest in candid, confidential deliberations within the Executive Branch. [The] standards proposed by the President and the Solicitor General—if applied outside the context of privileged information—would risk seriously impeding Congress in carrying out its responsibilities. The President and the Solicitor General would apply the same exacting standards to *all* subpoenas for the President's information, without recognizing distinctions between privileged and nonprivileged information, between official and personal information, or between various legislative objectives. Such a categorical approach would represent a significant departure from the longstanding way of doing business between the branches, giving short shrift to Congress's important interests in conducting inquiries to obtain the information it needs to legislate effectively.

"[The] House meanwhile would have us ignore that these suits involve the President. Invoking our precedents concerning investigations that did not target the President's papers, the House urges us to uphold its subpoenas because they relate to a valid legislative purpose or concern a subject on which legislation could be had [citations and internal quotation marks omitted]. Far from accounting for separation of powers concerns, the House's approach aggravates them by leaving essentially no limits on the congressional power to subpoena the President's personal records. Any personal paper possessed by a President could potentially 'relate to' a conceivable subject of legislation, for Congress has broad legislative powers that touch a vast number of subjects. The President's financial records could relate to economic reform, medical records to health reform, school transcripts to education reform, and so on.

Indeed, at argument, the House was unable to identify *any* type of information that lacks some relation to potential legislation.

"[Congressional] subpoenas for the President's personal information implicate weighty concerns regarding the separation of powers. Neither side, however, identifies an approach that accounts for these concerns. [A] balanced approach is necessary. [First,] courts should carefully assess whether the asserted legislative purpose warrants the significant step of involving the President and his papers. [Congress] may not rely on the President's information if other sources could reasonably provide Congress the information it needs in light of its particular legislative objective. [Second], to narrow the scope of possible conflict between the branches, courts should insist on a subpoena no broader than reasonably necessary to support Congress's legislative objective. [Third], courts should be attentive to the nature of the evidence offered by Congress to establish that a subpoena advances a valid legislative purpose. The more detailed and substantial the evidence of Congress's legislative purpose, the better. [Fourth], courts should be careful to assess the burdens imposed on the President by a subpoena. [Other] considerations may be pertinent as well; one case every two centuries does not afford enough experience for an exhaustive list." The Court remanded for application of the foregoing criteria.

THOMAS, J., dissented: "I would hold that Congress has no power to issue a legislative subpoena for private, nonofficial documents—whether they belong to the President or not. Congress may be able to obtain these documents as part of an investigation of the President, but to do so, it must proceed under the impeachment power."

ALITO, J., also dissented. Although he assumed *arguendo* that Congress may issue a subpoena to the President in the exercise of its legislative powers in some circumstances, he thought the Court's conditions were too permissive. He contended that "the House should provide a description of the type of legislation being considered, and while great specificity is not necessary, the description should be sufficient to permit a court to assess whether the particular records sought are of any special importance. The House should also spell out its constitutional authority to enact the type of legislation that it is contemplating, and it should justify the scope of the subpoenas in relation to the articulated legislative needs. In addition, it should explain why the subpoenaed information, as opposed to information available from other sources, is needed. Unless the House is required to make a showing along these lines, I would hold that enforcement of the subpoenas cannot be ordered."

4. IMPEACHMENT OF THE PRESIDENT

P. 268, replace the introductory paragraph to Section 4 with the following:

In December 2019, for the third time in U.S. history, the House of Representatives impeached the President, who was then tried by the

Senate. In January 2021, with just days remaining in his Term, President Donald Trump was impeached a second time. In each instance—Andrew Johnson in 1868, William Clinton in 1999, and Trump in 2020 and again in 2021—the Senate voted to acquit. A fourth President, Richard Nixon, would almost certainly have been impeached and very likely convicted and removed had he not resigned in 1974. In *Nixon v. United States* Ch. 1, Sec. 2 *supra*, (which concerned a federal judge with the same surname as the former President) the Supreme Court ruled that matters respecting congressional impeachments present nonjusticiable political questions. Thus, no judicial opinions address any of the important constitutional questions that may arise. The following notes consider some of these:

P. 271, add the following at the end of the chapter:

4.   *Disqualification of former officers.* One week before President Trump was scheduled to leave office, the House of Representatives impeached him for "incitement of insurrection" by encouraging his supporters to storm the Capitol while Congress was engaged in the ordinarily ceremonial function of counting Electoral College votes. The Senate trial did not occur until February 2021, after a new President had been inaugurated. Relying on various early precedents, including the British Parliament's impeachment of Warren Hastings two years after his resignation as Governor General of Bengal, House managers argued that former officials remain subject to impeachment. Conviction, they said, was necessary to disqualify Trump from holding future federal office, including the Presidency. Many of the Senators who voted to acquit argued that disqualification can be an incident of conviction but that a former President cannot be tried on impeachment charges, which are available only for sitting officers. Does the text of the Constitution speak clearly to the permissibility of impeaching former officers? If the Senate had convicted and disqualified President Trump from future office holding but he nonetheless ran for President again, what person or body would have responsibility for determining his eligibility? Recall that *Nixon v. United States* [Ch. 1, Sec. 2] holds that a challenge to a judgment of impeachment presents a non-justiciable political question, placing special reliance on the difficulties that would ensue were a Presidential impeachment subject to judicial review. In light of *Nixon*, can courts hear a case seeking to *enforce* a Senate judgment of ineligibility following impeachment?

CHAPTER 4

STATE POWER TO REGULATE

∎ ∎ ∎

2. BASIC DOCTRINAL PRINCIPLES AND THEIR APPLICATION

I. STATUTES THAT DISCRIMINATE ON THEIR FACES AGAINST INTERSTATE COMMERCE

P. 289, before *Maine v. Taylor*:

TENNESSEE WINE AND SPIRITS RETAILERS ASS'N v. TENNESSEE ALCOHOLIC BEVERAGE COMM'N, 139 S.Ct. 2449 (2019), invalidated a Tennessee statute that imposed a two-year duration-of-residency requirement for licenses to own and operate liquor stores. Writing for a 7–2 majority, ALITO, J., began by noting recent criticisms of dormant Commerce Clause doctrine, but he responded by citing original historical expectations that the Constitution would provide "protection against a broad swathe of state protectionist measures." Within the existing doctrinal framework, Tennessee's principal defense of its discriminatory residency test rested on § 2 of the Twenty-first Amendment, which provides that "[t]he transportation or importation into any State, Territory, or possession of the United States for delivery or use therein of intoxicating liquors, in violation of the laws thereof, is hereby prohibited." Despite some early judicial suggestions that § 2 gave the states plenary control over all matters involving alcohol, the Court had subsequently recognized that it must "scrutinize state alcohol laws for compliance with many constitutional provisions," including the First and Fourteenth Amendments. With respect to the dormant Commerce Clause, examination of relevant history "convince[s] us that the aim of § 2 was not to give states a free hand to restrict the importation of alcohol." GORSUCH, J., joined by Thomas, J., dissented: "[T]hose who ratified the [Twenty-first] Amendment wanted the States to be able to regulate the sale of liquor free of judicial meddling under the dormant Commerce Clause."

① discriminate on their faces.
rationale: historical expectations of
the constitution to protect against
state protectionist measures.
holding: the aim of §2 of 21ˢᵗ Amend.
was not to give states a free hand to
restrict the importation of alcohol.

CHAPTER 5

SUBSTANTIVE PROTECTION OF ECONOMIC INTERESTS

■ ■ ■

4. OTHER LIMITS ON ECONOMIC LEGISLATION: THE PROHIBITION AGAINST "TAKING" "PRIVATE PROPERTY" WITHOUT JUST COMPENSATION

P. 398, replace the first two paragraphs (on *Horne*) with:

In CEDAR POINT NURSERY v. HASID, 141 S.Ct. 2063 (2021), ROBERTS, C.J., wrote for the Court that a California regulation granting union organizers access to private agricultural property "for up to three hours per day, 120 days per year" was a physical invasion subject to *Loretto*'s *per se* rule: "Government action that physically appropriates property is no less a physical taking because it arises from a regulation. [The] essential question [is] whether the government has physically taken property for itself or someone else—by whatever means—or has instead restricted a property owner's ability to use his own property. Whenever a regulation results in a physical appropriation of property, a *per se* taking has occurred, and *Penn Central* has no place. [The] regulation grants union organizers a right to physically enter and occupy the growers' land for three hours per day, 120 days per year. Rather than restraining the growers' use of their own property, the regulation appropriates for the enjoyment of third parties the owners' right to exclude. [The] duration of an appropriation—just like the size of an appropriation, see Loretto,—bears only on the amount of compensation."

BREYER, J., joined by Sotomayor and Kagan, JJ., dissented on the ground that the "regulation does not 'appropriate' anything; it regulates the employers' right to exclude others. [The] 'access' that it grants union organizers does not amount to any traditional property interest in land. [It] gives union organizers the right temporarily to invade a portion of the property owners' land. It thereby limits the landowners' right to exclude certain others. The regulation *regulates* (but does not *appropriate*) the owners' right to exclude." Thus, according to the dissent, the majority had disregarded *Loretto*'s distinction between "permanent physical occupations" and "temporary limitations on the right to exclude."

CHAPTER 6

PROTECTION OF INDIVIDUAL RIGHTS: DUE PROCESS, THE BILL OF RIGHTS, AND UNENUMERATED RIGHTS

■ ■ ■

1. APPLICABILITY OF THE BILL OF RIGHTS TO THE STATES; NATURE AND SCOPE OF FOURTEENTH AMENDMENT DUE PROCESS

II. IS THE BILL OF RIGHTS INCORPORATED "JOT-FOR-JOT"?

Pp. 418–20, delete the note on *Baldwin, Williams,* and *Apodaca.*

III. IN *MCDONALD V. CITY OF CHICAGO,* THE COURT LOOKS BACK ON ITS "INCORPORATION" OF BILL OF RIGHTS GUARANTEES

P. 421, delete footnote 14 and insert immediately before IV:

In TIMBS v. INDIANA, 139 S.Ct. 682 (2019), GINSBURG, J., wrote for the Court that "the historical and logical case for concluding that the Fourteenth Amendment incorporates the Excessive Fines Clause is overwhelming." The Court rejected the State's contention that the Fourteenth Amendment did not incorporate the Clause's application to civil *in rem* forfeitures that are at least partly punitive. The decision was unanimous in result, but THOMAS, J., concurred only in the judgment. Adhering to a view he expressed in *McDonald* (Sec. 7 *infra*), he would have relied on the Fourteenth Amendment's Privileges or Immunities Clause as the basis for incorporation. Concurring in the majority opinion, GORSUCH, J., "acknowledge[d]" that "[a]s an original matter ... the appropriate vehicle for incorporation may well be the Fourteenth Amendment's Privileges or Immunities Clause, rather than, as this Court has long assumed, the Due Process Clause." However, he continued, "nothing in this case turns on that question, and, regardless of the precise vehicle, there can be no serious doubt that the Fourteenth Amendment requires the States to respect the freedom from excessive fines enshrined in the Eighth Amendment."

RAMOS v. LOUISIANA, 140 S.Ct. 1390 (2020), presented the question whether the Sixth Amendment requirement of a unanimous twelve-person jury in serious criminal cases is incorporated. GORSUCH, J., wrote for the Court: "In 48 States and federal court, a single juror's vote to acquit is enough to prevent a conviction. But not in Louisiana. Along with Oregon, Louisiana has long punished people based on 10-to-2 verdicts. [Wherever] we might look to determine what the term 'trial by an impartial jury trial' meant at the time of the Sixth Amendment's adoption—whether it's the common law, state practices in the founding era, or opinions and treatises written soon afterward—the answer is unmistakable. A jury must reach a unanimous verdict in order to convict.

"There can be no question either that the Sixth Amendment's unanimity requirement applies to state and federal criminal trials equally. This Court has long explained that the Sixth Amendment right to a jury trial is 'fundamental to the American scheme of justice' and incorporated against the States under the Fourteenth Amendment. This Court has long explained, too, that incorporated provisions of the Bill of Rights bear the same content when asserted against States as they do when asserted against the federal government. So if the Sixth Amendment's right to a jury trial requires a unanimous verdict to support a conviction in federal court, it requires no less in state court.

"How, despite these seemingly straightforward principles, have Louisiana's and Oregon's laws managed to hang on for so long? It turns out that the Sixth Amendment's otherwise simple story took a strange turn. [In] *Apodaca v. Oregon*, 406 U.S. 404 (1972), [four] dissenting Justices would not have hesitated to strike down the States' laws, recognizing that the Sixth Amendment requires unanimity and that this guarantee is fully applicable against the States under the Fourteenth Amendment. But a four-Justice plurality [declared] that the real question [was] whether unanimity serves an important 'function' in 'contemporary society.' [Justice] Powell agreed that, as a matter of 'history and precedent, the Sixth Amendment requires a unanimous jury verdict to convict.' But, on the other hand, he argued that the Fourteenth Amendment does not render this guarantee against the federal government fully applicable against the States. In this way, Justice Powell doubled down on his belief in 'dual-track' incorporation—the idea that a single right can mean two different things depending on whether it is being invoked against the federal or a state government.

"[Even] if we accepted the premise that *Apodaca* established a precedent, no one on the Court today is prepared to say it was rightly decided, and *stare decisis* isn't supposed to be the art of methodically ignoring what everyone knows to be true. [Louisiana and Oregon] credibly claim that the number of nonunanimous felony convictions still on direct appeal are somewhere in the hundreds, and retrying or plea bargaining these cases will surely impose a cost. But new rules of criminal procedures usually do, often affecting significant numbers of pending cases across the whole country."

SOTOMAYOR and KAVANAUGH, JJ., each wrote a partial concurrence explaining their respective views of *stare decisis*. THOMAS, J., concurred in the judgment, reiterating his view that the Fourteenth Amendment's Privileges or Immunities Clause provides the proper basis for incorporation. *See McDonald, infra*, Sec. 7.

ALITO, J., joined by Roberts, C.J., and Kagan, J., dissented on *stare decisis* grounds: The Court "imposes a potentially crushing burden on the courts and criminal justice systems of [Louisiana and Oregon]. Whatever one may think about the correctness of [*Apodaca*], it has elicited enormous and entirely reasonable reliance. And before this Court decided to intervene, the decision appeared to have little practical importance going forward. Louisiana has now abolished non-unanimous verdicts, and Oregon seemed on the verge of doing the same until the Court intervened."

IV. HOW MUCH MORE SPECIFIC ARE PROVISIONS OF THE BILL OF RIGHTS THAN DUE PROCESS GENERALLY? THE CASE OF BODILY EXTRACTIONS

P. 425, at the end of note 2:

3. *Mandatory vaccination.* As this Supplement went to press in summer 2021, three safe and effective vaccines for COVID-19 had received emergency use authorization and were widely available for free in the United States. However, some vulnerable people are unable to receive the vaccine due to underlying medical conditions. Nonetheless, unvaccinated individuals can be protected by a vaccine administered to others through *herd immunity*: when a sufficiently high proportion of the community has been vaccinated or acquired immunity from the disease itself, the contagion ceases to spread because it does not encounter sufficiently many vulnerable hosts. The portion of the population that must be vaccinated for a community to achieve herd immunity depends on the vaccine's effectiveness and the disease's contagiousness. Given that substantial numbers of Americans without any underlying medical condition have declined to be vaccinated, herd immunity against COVID-19 might not be achieved. Even if it is, herd immunity might be unachievable against other deadly diseases without a government vaccination mandate. Would such a mandate violate a right to bodily autonomy?

JACOBSON v. MASSACHUSETTS, 197 U.S. 11 (1905), per HARLAN, J., upheld a criminal conviction of the defendant for refusal to submit to a free state-mandated vaccination against smallpox: The defendant relied on "the general theory of those of the medical profession who attach little or no value to vaccination as a means of preventing the spread of smallpox, or who think that vaccination causes other diseases of the body. What everybody knows, the court must know, and therefore the state court judicially knew, as this court knows, that an opposite theory accords with the common belief and is maintained by high medical authority. We must assume that, when the statute in question was passed, the legislature of Massachusetts was not unaware of these opposing theories, and was compelled, of necessity, to choose between them. [The] state legislature proceeded upon the theory which recognized vaccination as at least an effective, if not the best, known way in which to meet and suppress the evils of a smallpox epidemic that imperiled an entire population. [Whatever] may be thought of the expediency of this statute, it cannot be affirmed to be, beyond question, in palpable conflict with the Constitution. Nor, in view of the methods employed to stamp out the disease of smallpox, can anyone confidently assert that the means prescribed by the State to that end has no real or substantial relation to the protection of the public health and the public safety."

Note that *Jacobson* was decided in the same year as *Lochner*, whose author, Peckham, J., along with Brewer, J., dissented without opinion. Does *Jacobson* apply the same test as modern bodily autonomy cases? If not, is it nonetheless still good law?

2. REPRODUCTIVE FREEDOM

Introductory Note on the Right of "Privacy"

P. 442, at the end of footnote 14:

McCorvey's story took one final surprise turn. Before her death in February 2017, she issued what she sardonically called a "deathbed confession" that she was never really pro-life after all. Footage was included in a television documentary that premiered on the FX Network in 2020. *AKA Jane Roe* also showed financial records indicating that McCorvey had been paid nearly half a million dollars by pro-life organizations and individuals.

The Court Reaffirms "the Essential Holding of *Roe*"

P. 472, at the end of note 5:

In DOBBS v. JACKSON WOMEN'S HEALTH, *cert. granted*, 2021 WL 1951792 (2021), the Court will consider the constitutionality of a Mississippi statute barring most abortions after 15 weeks of pregnancy. Although the petition presented three questions, the Court granted review on only one: "Whether all pre-viability prohibitions on elective abortions are unconstitutional."

Purported Health Regulations

P. 484, at the end of note 2:

3. ***Balancing and stare decisis (revisited).*** According to the *Whole Woman's Health* majority, *Casey* "requires that courts consider the burdens a law imposes on abortion access together with the benefits those laws confer" in determining whether the former are "undue." Does *Casey* as construed by *Whole Woman's Health* thus establish a balancing test? That question divided the Court in JUNE MEDICAL SERVICES L. L. C. v. RUSSO, 140 S.Ct. 2103 (2020). BREYER, J., again delivered the judgment, although here, unlike in *Whole Woman's Health*, he spoke only for a plurality consisting of himself and Ginsburg, Sotomayor, and Kagan, JJ.

The Court considered "the constitutionality of a Louisiana statute, Act 620, that is almost word-for-word identical to Texas' admitting-privileges law. As in *Whole Woman's Health*, the District Court found that the statute offers no significant health benefit. It found that conditions on admitting privileges common to hospitals throughout the State have made and will continue to make it impossible for abortion providers to obtain conforming privileges for reasons that have nothing to do with the State's asserted interests in promoting women's health and safety. And it found that this inability places a substantial obstacle in the path of women seeking an abortion. As in *Whole Woman's Health*, the substantial obstacle the Act imposes, and the absence of any health-related benefit, led the District Court to conclude that the law imposes an undue burden and is therefore unconstitutional." Because the appeals court nonetheless found distinctions between the Louisiana and Texas laws in their application, it upheld Act 620. The Court reversed, invalidating it as indistinguishable from the Texas law.

Crediting the district court's factual findings as not clearly erroneous, the plurality observed that Act 620 "would leave Louisiana with just one clinic with one provider to serve the 10,000 women annually who seek abortions in the State. Working full time in New Orleans, [that one doctor, identified in the record as] Doe 5 would be able to absorb no more than about 30% of the annual demand for abortions in Louisiana. And because Doe 5 does not perform abortions beyond 18 weeks, women between 18 weeks and the state legal limit of 20 weeks would have little or no way to exercise their constitutional right to an abortion.

"Those women not altogether prevented from obtaining an abortion would face other burdens. As in *Whole Woman's Health*, the reduction in abortion providers caused by Act 620 would inevitably mean 'longer waiting times, and increased crowding.' The District Court heard testimony that delays in obtaining an abortion increase the risk that a woman will experience complications from the procedure and may make it impossible for her to choose a noninvasive medication abortion.

"Even if they obtain an appointment at a clinic, women who might previously have gone to a clinic in Baton Rouge or Shreveport would face increased driving distances. New Orleans is nearly a five hour drive from Shreveport; it is over an hour from Baton Rouge; and Baton Rouge is more than four hours from Shreveport. The impact of those increases would be magnified by Louisiana's requirement that every woman undergo an ultrasound and receive mandatory counseling at least 24 hours before an abortion. A Shreveport resident seeking an abortion who might previously have obtained care at one of that city's local clinics would either have to spend nearly 20 hours driving back and forth to Doe 5's clinic twice, or else find overnight lodging in New Orleans. As the District Court stated, both experts and laypersons testified that the burdens of this increased travel would fall disproportionately on poor women, who are least able to absorb them.

"[The] District Court found that the admitting-privileges requirement serves no 'relevant credentialing function.' [H]ospitals can, and do, deny admitting privileges for reasons unrelated to a doctor's ability safely to perform abortions. And Act 620's requirement that physicians obtain privileges at a hospital within 30 miles of the place where they perform abortions further constrains providers for reasons that bear no relationship to competence. [Further,] the District Court found that the admitting-privileges requirement 'does not conform to prevailing medical standards and will not improve the safety of abortion in Louisiana.' As in *Whole Woman's Health*, the [State] introduced no evidence 'showing that patients have better outcomes when their physicians have admitting privileges' or 'of any instance in which an admitting privileges requirement would have helped even one woman obtain better treatment.'

"[This] case is similar to, nearly identical with, *Whole Woman's Health*. And the law must consequently reach a similar conclusion. Act 620 is unconstitutional."

ROBERTS, C.J., concurred in the judgment: "I joined the dissent in *Whole Woman's Health* and continue to believe that the case was wrongly decided. The question today however is not whether *Whole Woman's Health* was right or wrong, but whether to adhere to it in deciding the present case. [The] legal doctrine of *stare decisis* requires us, absent special circumstances, to treat like cases alike. The Louisiana law imposes a burden on access to abortion just as severe as that imposed by the Texas law, for the same reasons. Therefore Louisiana's law cannot stand under our precedents.

"*Stare decisis* ('to stand by things decided') is the legal term for fidelity to precedent. Black's Law Dictionary 1696 (11th ed. 2019). It has long been "an established rule to abide by former precedents, where the same points come again in litigation; as well to keep the scale of justice even and steady, and not liable to waver with every new judge's opinion.' 1 W. Blackstone, Commentaries on the Laws of England 69 (1765). This principle is grounded in a basic humility that recognizes today's legal issues are often not so different from the questions of yesterday and that we are not the first ones to try to answer them. Because the 'private stock of reason . . . in each man is small, . . . individuals would do better to avail themselves of the general bank and capital of nations and of ages.' 3 Edmund Burke, *Reflections on the Revolution in France* 110 (1790).

"Adherence to precedent is necessary to 'avoid an arbitrary discretion in the courts.' *The Federalist* No. 78, p. 529 (J. Cooke ed. 1961) (A. Hamilton). The constraint of precedent distinguishes the judicial "method and philosophy from those of the political and legislative process." Robert Jackson, *Decisional Law and Stare Decisis*, 30 A.B.A.J. 334 (1944).

"The doctrine also brings pragmatic benefits. Respect for precedent 'promotes the evenhanded, predictable, and consistent development of legal principles, fosters reliance on judicial decisions, and contributes to the actual and perceived integrity of the judicial process.' *Payne v. Tennessee*, 501 U.S. 808 (1991). It is the 'means by which we ensure that the law will not merely change erratically, but will develop in a principled and intelligible fashion.' *Vasquez v. Hillery*, 474 U.S. 254 (1986). In that way, 'stare decisis is an old friend of the common lawyer.' Jackson, *supra*.

"*Stare decisis* is not an 'inexorable command.' *Ramos* v. *Louisiana, supra* (internal quotation marks omitted). But for precedent to mean anything, the doctrine must give way only to a rationale that goes beyond whether the case was decided correctly. The Court accordingly considers additional factors before overruling a precedent, such as its administrability, its fit with subsequent factual and legal developments, and the reliance interests that the precedent has engendered.

"*Stare decisis* principles also determine how we handle a decision that itself departed from the cases that came before it. In those instances, '[r]emaining true to an 'intrinsically sounder' doctrine established in prior cases better serves the values of *stare decisis* than would following' the recent departure. *Adarand Constructors, Inc.* v. *Peña*, Ch.9, Sec. 2, V(A) (plurality opinion). *Stare decisis* is pragmatic and contextual, not 'a mechanical formula of adherence to the latest decision.' *Helvering v. Hallock*, 309 U.S. 106 (1940).

"[The parties] agree that the undue burden standard announced in *Casey* provides the appropriate framework to analyze Louisiana's law. Neither party has asked us to reassess the constitutional validity of that standard. [Under] *Casey*, the State may not impose an undue burden on the woman's ability to obtain an abortion.

"[The] Court in *Whole Woman's Health* added the following observation [to its recitation of the *Casey* standard]: 'The rule announced in *Casey* . . . requires that courts consider the burdens a law imposes on abortion access together with the benefits those laws confer.' The plurality repeats today that the undue burden standard requires courts 'to weigh the law's asserted benefits against the burdens it imposes on abortion access.'

"[Under] such [grand balancing] tests, 'equality of treatment is . . . impossible to achieve; predictability is destroyed; judicial arbitrariness is facilitated; judicial courage is impaired.' Antonin Scalia, *The Rule of Law as a Law of Rules*, 56 U.Chi.L.Rev. 1175 (1989). In this context, courts applying a balancing test would be asked in essence to weigh the State's interests in 'protecting the potentiality of human life' and the health of the woman, on the one hand, against the woman's liberty interest in defining her 'own concept of existence, of meaning, of the universe, and of the mystery of human life' on the other. *Casey*. There is no plausible sense in which anyone, let alone this Court, could objectively assign weight to such imponderable values and no meaningful way to compare them if there were.

"[Nothing] about *Casey* suggested that a weighing of costs and benefits of an abortion regulation was a job for the courts. [The] upshot of *Casey* is clear: The several restrictions that did not impose a substantial obstacle were constitutional, while the restriction that did impose a substantial obstacle was unconstitutional. To be sure, the Court at times discussed the benefits of the regulations, including when it distinguished spousal notification from parental consent. But in the context of *Casey*'s governing standard, these benefits were not placed on a scale opposite the law's burdens. Rather, *Casey* discussed benefits in considering the threshold requirement that the State have a 'legitimate purpose' and that the law be 'reasonably related to that goal.' So long as that showing is made, the only question for a court is whether a law has the 'effect of placing a substantial obstacle in the path of a woman seeking an abortion of a nonviable fetus.' *Casey* repeats that 'substantial obstacle' standard nearly verbatim no less than 15 times.

"[Nonetheless, w]e should respect the statement in *Whole Woman's Health* that it was applying the undue burden standard of *Casey*. [Here] the plurality expressly acknowledges that we are not considering how to analyze an abortion regulation that does not present a substantial obstacle. [In] this case, *Casey*'s requirement of finding a substantial obstacle before invalidating an abortion regulation is therefore a sufficient basis for the decision, as it was in *Whole Woman's Health*. In neither case, nor in *Casey* itself, was there call for consideration of a regulation's benefits, and nothing in *Casey* commands such consideration. Under principles of *stare decisis*, I agree with the plurality that the determination in *Whole Woman's Health* that Texas's law imposed a substantial obstacle requires the same determination about Louisiana's law. Under those same principles, I would adhere to the holding of *Casey*, requiring a substantial obstacle before striking down an abortion regulation."

THOMAS, J., dissented chiefly on the ground that the plaintiffs should be denied third-party standing. On the merits, he added that the Court's abortion "decisions created the right to abortion out of whole cloth, without a shred of support from the Constitution's text. Our abortion precedents are grievously wrong and should be overruled."

ALITO, J., joined in full by Gorsuch, J., and in different parts by Thomas and Kavanaugh, JJ., dissented. In portions of his dissent in which all the dissenters concurred, he agreed with Chief Justice Roberts that *Casey* "rules out the balancing test adopted in *Whole Woman's Health*. *Whole Woman's*

Health simply misinterpreted *Casey* [and] should be overruled insofar as it changed the *Casey* test. Unless *Casey* is reexamined—and Louisiana has not asked us to do that—the test it adopted should remain the governing standard.

"[In] any event, contrary to the view taken by the plurality and (seemingly) by the Chief Justice, there is ample evidence in the record showing that admitting privileges help to protect the health of women by ensuring that physicians who perform abortions meet a higher standard of competence than is shown by the mere possession of a license to practice. In deciding whether to grant admitting privileges, hospitals typically undertake a rigorous investigative process to ensure that a doctor is responsible and competent and has the training and experience needed to perform the procedures for which the privileges are sought. [Both] the plurality and the Chief Justice err in concluding that the admitting-privileges requirement serves no valid purpose.

"They also err in their assessment of Act 620's likely effect on access to abortion. [Because] the Louisiana law was not allowed to go into effect for any appreciable time, it was necessary for the District Court to predict what its effects would be. Attempting to do that, the court apparently concluded that none of the doctors who currently perform abortions in the State would be replaced if the admitting privileges requirement forced them to leave abortion practice. [The] finding was based on a fundamentally flawed test. In attempting to ascertain how many of the doctors who perform abortions in the State would have to leave abortion practice for lack of admitting privileges, the District Court received evidence in a variety of forms—some live testimony, but also deposition transcripts, declarations, and even letters from counsel—about the doctors' unsuccessful efforts to obtain privileges. The District Court considered whether these doctors had proceeded in 'good faith'; it found that they all met that standard; and it therefore concluded that the law would leave the State with very few abortion providers. [However, w]hen the District Court made its assessment of the doctors' 'good faith,' enforcement of Act 620 had been preliminarily enjoined, and the doctors surely knew that enforcement would be permanently barred if the lawsuit was successful. Thus, the doctors had everything to lose and nothing to gain by obtaining privileges."

GORSUCH, J., dissented on multiple grounds, including an objection that in crediting the district court's findings, the Court slighted the state legislature: "Act 620's admitting privileges requirement for abortion providers tracks longstanding state laws governing physicians who perform relatively low-risk procedures like colonoscopies, Lasik eye surgeries, and steroid injections at ambulatory surgical centers. In fact, the Louisiana legislature passed Act 620 only after extensive hearings at which experts detailed how the Act would promote safer abortion treatment—by providing 'a more thorough evaluation mechanism of physician competency,' promoting 'continuity of care' following abortion, enhancing inter-physician communication, and preventing patient abandonment."

Agreeing with the Chief Justice regarding balancing, Justice Gorsuch added that "the legal standard the plurality applies when it comes to admitting privileges for abortion clinics turns out to be exactly the sort of all-things-considered balancing of benefits and burdens this Court has long rejected. Really, it's little more than the judicial version of a hunter's stew: Throw in anything that looks interesting, stir, and season to taste.

"[The] plurality sides with the district court in concluding that the time and cost some women might have to endure to obtain an abortion outweighs the benefits of Act 620. Perhaps the plurality sees that answer as obvious, given its apparent conclusion that the Act would offer the public no benefits of any kind. But for its test to provide any helpful guidance, it must be capable of resolving cases the plurality can't so easily dismiss. Suppose, for example, a factfinder credited the State's evidence of medical benefit, finding that a small number of women would obtain safer medical care if the law went into effect. But suppose the same factfinder *also* credited a plaintiff's evidence of burden, finding that a large number of women would have to endure longer wait times and farther drives, and that a very small number of women would be unable to obtain an abortion at all. How is a judge supposed to balance, say, a few women's emergency hysterectomies against many women spending extra hours travelling to a clinic? The plurality's test offers no guidance. Nor can it. The benefits and burdens are incommensurable, and they do not teach such things in law school."

KAVANAUGH, J., also briefly dissented separately, expressing agreement with the conclusion of Justice Alito "that the Court should remand the case for a new trial and additional factfinding under the appropriate legal standards."

7. THE RIGHT TO KEEP AND BEAR ARMS

P. 587, immediately before Section 8:

NEW YORK STATE RIFLE & PISTOL ASS'N v. CITY OF NEW YORK, 140 S.Ct. 1525 (2020), involved a challenge to a New York City rule restricting the transport of firearms outside of the city, including to shooting ranges and competitions. The city changed the rule before the case reached the Supreme Court, which accordingly dismissed the case as moot in a brief *per curiam* opinion.

ALITO, J., joined by Gorsuch and Thomas, JJ., dissented and would have reached the merits: "We deal here with the same core Second Amendment right [recognized in *Heller* and *McDonald*], the right to keep a handgun in the home for self-defense. [A] necessary concomitant of this right is the right to take a gun outside the home for certain purposes. One of these is to take a gun for maintenance or repair. [Another] is to take a gun outside the home in order to transfer ownership lawfully. [And] still another is to take a gun to a range in order to gain and maintain the skill necessary to use it responsibly."

KAVANAUGH, J., agreed with the *per curiam*'s mootness holding, but concurred to express agreement as well with the dissent's discussion of the merits: "I share Justice Alito's concern that some federal and state courts may not be properly applying *Heller* and *McDonald*. The Court should address that issue soon . . . ."

In NEW YORK STATE RIFLE v. CORLETT, *cert. granted*, 2021 WL 1602643 (2021), the Court will consider whether the state's denial of "applications for concealed-carry licenses for self-defense violated the Second Amendment."

8. THE DEATH PENALTY AND RELATED PROBLEMS: CRUEL AND UNUSUAL PUNISHMENT

IV. ADDITIONAL CONSTITUTIONAL LIMITS ON IMPOSING SEVERE PUNISHMENT

P. 608, after the final paragraph:

In FORD v. WAINWRIGHT, 477 U.S. 399 (1986), the Supreme Court, per MARSHALL, J., held that the Eighth Amendment forbids executing a prisoner who has "lost his sanity" after sentencing. In MADISON v. ALABAMA, 139 S.Ct. 718 (2019), a 5–3 majority of the Court, per KAGAN, J., applied *Ford* in holding that a prisoner's mere failure to remember committing his crime does not preclude execution but dementia that renders him "unable to rationally understand the reasons for his sentence" does. The Court remanded for application of this standard. ALITO, J., joined by Thomas and Gorsuch, JJ., dissented on the grounds that only the memory question was properly before the Court and that, in any event, the state court had applied the correct standard to the dementia question.

P. 611, after the first full paragraph:

In JONES v. MISSISSIPPI, 141 S.Ct. 1307 (2021), KAVANAUGH, J., in an opinion for the Court, concluded that a juvenile's sentence of LWOP complies with *Miller* so long as the judge acknowledges discretion to impose a lesser sentence, even without making a factual finding that the defendant is permanently incorrigible. SOTOMAYOR, J., joined by Breyer and Kagan, JJ., dissented, arguing that the majority's ruling failed to honor *Miller*'s requirement that a sentencing court offer an individualized reason to conclude that the particular defendant lacks the "distinctive attributes of youth [that] diminish the penological justifications for imposing the harshest sentences on juvenile offenders, even when they commit terrible crimes."

P. 614, before Section 9:

In BUCKLEW v. PRECYTHE, 139 S.Ct. 1112 (2019), a prisoner argued that Missouri's one-drug protocol would be unconstitutional as applied to him because vascular tumors in his head, neck, and throat posed a substantial risk of excruciating pain during the execution. GORSUCH, J., writing for a 5–4 Court, rejected the claim on the ground that in as-applied no less than facial challenges to a method of execution the challenger bears the burden of identifying a " 'feasible, readily implemented' alternative procedure that would 'significantly reduce a substantial risk of severe pain' " (quoting *Glossip* plurality opinion). According to the majority, execution by nitrogen hypoxia, the alternative method to which the prisoner eventually pointed, did not satisfy this standard. BREYER, J., joined by Ginsburg, Sotomayor, and Kagan, JJ., dissented on multiple grounds, including the contention that as-applied challenges should be treated differently from facial ones because the former do not undercut any legislative judgment: "It is impossible to believe that Missouri's legislature, when adopting lethal injection, considered the possibility that it would cause prisoners to choke on their own blood for up to several minutes before they die."

CHAPTER 7

FREEDOM OF EXPRESSION
AND ASSOCIATION

■ ■ ■

1. THE SCOPE AND STRENGTH OF
THE FIRST AMENDMENT

I. ADVOCACY OF ILLEGAL ACTION

D. A Modern "Restatement"

P. 680, at the end of note 8:

In NIEVES v. BARTLETT, 139 S.Ct. 1715 (2019), the Court seemingly narrowed its conclusion in *Lozman*. In *Nieves*, Russell Bartlett had been arrested for disorderly conduct and resisting arrest in the context of an altercation that took place during an Alaska sports festival "known for both extreme sports and extreme alcohol consumption." The criminal charges against Bartlett were ultimately dismissed, whereupon he sued the arresting officers, including Nieves, under 42 U.S.C. § 1983, claiming that his arrest was in retaliation for his speech, in particular his comments during the altercation about the behavior of the arresting officers. The district court having determined that the officers had probable cause to arrest Bartlett, the issue then turned on the question of the burden of proof in a retaliatory arrest claim based on an allegation that the arrest was in retaliation for engaging in otherwise protected speech.

Writing for the Court, ROBERTS, C.J., noted that *Lozman* was based on "unusual circumstances" and that *Nieves v. Bartlett* presented a "more representative case." And in this more representative case, the Court concluded that the plaintiff must establish a causal connection between the impermissible retaliatory motive and the subsequent arrest, and that the causal connection must be of the "but for" variety. Noting that "protected speech is often a legitimate consideration when deciding whether to make an arrest," the Court concluded that the presence of probable cause would generally (*Lozman* presenting the narrow exception of the presence of probable cause under circumstances in which it could objectively be shown that otherwise similarly situated individuals not engaged in protected speech would not have been arrested) defeat a retaliatory arrest claim. When there was no probable cause for the arrest, it would still be necessary for the plaintiff to show that the retaliation was a "substantial or motivating factor behind the arrest." If a plaintiff were able to make such a showing, then the burden of proof would shift to the defendant to show that the arrest would have been initiated without respect to the retaliation.

THOMAS, J., concurring in part and concurring in the judgment, would have rejected even the *Lozman* exception. GORSUCH, J., concurring in part and dissenting in part, stressed that for him the presence of probable cause was relevant to a retaliatory arrest claim, but that it was not nearly as conclusive as it appeared to be for the majority. GINSBURG, J., concurring in part and dissenting in part, also objected to the weight given by the majority to the presence of probable cause. And SOTOMAYOR, J., dissenting, also took issue with the almost conclusive role the majority gave to the presence of probable cause, believing, with Ginsburg, J., that the proper approach was one drawn from *Mt. Healthy City Bd. of Educ. v. Doyle*, 429 U.S. 274 (1977), in which "the plaintiff bears the burden of demonstrating that unconstitutional animus was a motivating factor for an adverse action; the burden then shifts to the defendant to demonstrate that, even without any impetus to retaliate, the defendant would have taken the action complained of."

II. REPUTATION AND PRIVACY

B. Public Officials and Seditious Libel

P. 696, add as new note 6 after note 5:

6.   ***Challenging New York Times.*** In an era of social media, enhanced forms of electronic transmission, and the seeming accelerating proliferation of factual falsity, including demonstrable falsehoods about specific individuals, calls to reconsider *New York Times* have increased. On the desirability of fine-tuning around the edges in light of contemporary issues and technology, see David Logan, *Rescuing Our Democracy by Rethinking* New York Times v. Sullivan, 81 Ohio St. L.J. 759 (2020); Cass R. Sunstein, *Falsehoods and the First Amendment*, 33 Harv. J.L. & Tech. 388 (2020). And in opinions at the end of the 2020 Term dissenting from denials of certiorari in *Berisha v. Lawson*, 141 S.Ct. 2424 (2021), Justices Thomas and Gorsuch, in separate opinions, urged more substantial reconsideration of *New York Times*. Justice Thomas, echoing his earlier dissenting opinion in *McKee v. Cosby*, 139 S.Ct. 675 (2019) (Thomas, J., dissenting from the denial of certiorari), decried the full development of *New York Times v. Sullivan* and its progeny as departing from the historical understanding of the First Amendment and urged, more specifically, that its extension to public figures as well as public officials was especially problematic. And Justice Gorsuch, noting occasional academic questions about *New York Times* (including from then-Professor Elena Kagan), called more simply for reconsideration in light of the "real harm" that falsehoods about specific individuals could inflict and in light of the vast changes wrought by modern political and technological developments.

2. THE PROBLEM OF CONTENT REGULATION

P. 833, at the end of note 3:

Two Terms after *Matal v. Tam*, the Court revisited the issue of offensive trademarks in IANCU v. BRUNETTI, 139 S.Ct. 2294 (2019), where the Court held that the Lanham Act's prohibition on registration for "immoral or scandalous" trademarks constituted impermissible viewpoint-based discrimination. At issue was an attempted registration of the trademark FUCT by the clothing manufacturer who used these four letters, allegedly pronounced as four separate letters, as the brand name for its clothing line. Relying substantially on *Matal*, the Court, with KAGAN, J., writing the majority opinion, rejected the argument that the "immoral or scandalous" standard was merely a viewpoint-neutral restriction on the manner in which a point of view could be expressed but was not itself a viewpoint-based standard. The Court also rejected the government's argument that the statutory criteria were not facially invalid but only that there had been errors in application by trademark examiners in applying the criteria, and rejected as well the argument that the statute could be subject to a saving narrowing construction.

Concurring, ALITO, J., noted that a redrafted statute precluding registration of "vulgar terms" could likely be valid, but that "[v]iewpoint discrimination is poison to a free society. But in many countries with constitutions or legal traditions that claim to protect freedom of speech, serious viewpoint discrimination is now tolerated, and such discrimination has become increasingly prevalent in this country. At a time when free speech is under attack, it is especially important for this Court to remain firm on the principle that the First Amendment does not tolerate viewpoint discrimination."

ROBERTS, C.J., BREYER, J., and SOTOMAYOR, J., each wrote opinions concurring in part and dissenting in part. All three agreed with the majority that the "immoral" component in the statutory standard was impermissibly viewpoint-based, but that it could be excised by the Court, leaving the "scandalous" element in place, an element that for all three of these concurring justices was sufficiently close a restriction on only the lewd or the profane that it could be understood as not being viewpoint-based. Justice Breyer's opinion also objected to the Court's continuing reliance on rigid First Amendment categories, believing that the Court should focus on the "more basic proportionality question" whether the harm to the First Amendment's interests was disproportionate to the government's regulatory objectives.

I. "HATE SPEECH" AND THE *SKOKIE* CONTROVERSY

P. 882, after *Reed v. Gilbert*:

————

The Court's divisions about the scope and strength of the bar against content regulation continued in the 2019 Term. BARR v. AMERICAN

ASSOCIATION OF POLITICAL CONSULTANTS, INC., 140 S.Ct. 2335 (2020), produced a decision whose lack of a majority opinion underscored the way in which content regulation doctrine remains in flux and contested.

The case concerned the Telephone Consumer Protection Act of 1991, which in relevant part prohibits virtually all robocalls to cell phones. In 2015, however, Congress amended the Act to exclude from the robocall prohibition calls made to collect a government debt, a category including many student loans and home mortgages. An association of political consultants, many of whose members wished to be able to make political robocalls to cell phones, challenged the amended Act, arguing that its preference for government debt-collection robocalls over political robocalls violated the First Amendment.

In a fractured set of opinions, the Court agreed that the amended Act engaged in constitutionally impermissible content discrimination in violation of the First Amendment, and that the appropriate remedy, affirming the Fourth Circuit decision below, was to sever the constitutionally flawed government debt exception, leaving the overall robocall prohibition, without the exception, in place.

KAVANAUGH, J., writing for a plurality including himself, Roberts, C.J. Thomas, J. (in part), and Alito, J., relied heavily on *Reed* in concluding that the exception for government debt collection "impermissibly favored [government] debt-collection speech over political and other speech," and thus constituted unconstitutional content discrimination. Emphasizing that "content-based laws are subject to strict scrutiny," Justice Kavanaugh reiterated *Reed*'s conclusion that strict scrutiny applied to laws that "single[ ] out specific subject matter for differential treatment." For the plurality, the fact that the regulation was part of a broader regulatory scheme regulating the economic activity of debt collection was of no moment, because here the regulation of speech was not merely incidental to a broader regulatory program. Quoting *Sorrell v. IMS*, *supra*, Justice Kavanaugh argued that "the law here ['does] not simply have an effect on speech, but is directed at certain content and is aimed at particular speakers' "

Having concluded that strict scrutiny was the applicable standard, the merits of the controversy were essentially over, with even the government having conceded that "collecting government debt" was not the kind of interest that would satisfy strict scrutiny. But the question remained about the remedy. For the plurality, traditional severability principles were applicable, the most important of which, in this context, was the "presumption of severability." Applying that presumption and finding that the robocall prohibition without the government debt collection exception was "capable of functioning independently," *Murphy v. National Collegiate Athletic Association*, 138 S.Ct. 1461 (2018), the plurality held the unconstitutional exception severable, leaving the original exception-less robocall prohibition in place.

Much of the lack of a majority opinion was a function of the severability issue. GORSUCH, J., joined in part by Thomas, J., agreed with some of the plurality's analysis of the merits of the case but disagreed about severability. For Justice Gorsuch, the basic prohibition on robocalls to cell phones was itself an impermissible form of content regulation. As a result, he argued, severing the exception did not cure the basic problem, and he would have invalidated the entire prohibition. SOTOMAYOR, J., disagreed with the majority's content regulation analysis but concurred in the judgment because she agreed that the offending provision, if unconstitutional, was severable. BREYER, J., joined by Ginsburg and Kagan, JJ., reiterated his continuing concern with treating content regulation in almost all of its forms as triggering strict scrutiny. Although he consequently disagreed with the majority's view about the merits, he concurred in the judgment because he agreed that a provision that a majority of the Court had found constitutionally objectionable was severable from the entire statute.

4. NEW CATEGORIES?

I. HARM TO CHILDREN AND THE OVERBREADTH DOCTRINE

P. 923, add as new final paragraph to note 4:

Overbreadth doctrine remains both contested and misunderstood. In *Americans for Prosperity Foundation v. Bonta*, 141 S.Ct. 2373 (2021), discussed at length, *infra*, addition to p. 1162, the majority characterized as an overbreadth challenge what others would see simply as a facial challenge. Is a facial challenge, which, if successful, invalidates a statute in all of its applications, the same as an overbreadth challenge, as Roberts, C.J. seems to conclude in *Americans for Prosperity*, or is overbreadth merely a First-Amendment-specific standing doctrine applicable when a particular challenger who is not engaged in protected conduct challenges statute because it reaches the unprotected conduct of others?

7. GOVERNMENT SPEECH

II. GOVERNMENT AS EDUCATOR AND EDITOR

P. 1094, remove note 4 and add after note 3:

MAHANOY AREA SCHOOL DISTRICT V. B. L.

594 U.S. ___, 141 S.Ct. 2038, 206 L.Ed.2d ___ (2021).

JUSTICE BREYER delivered the opinion of the Court.

A public high school student used, and transmitted to her Snapchat friends, vulgar language and gestures criticizing both the school and the school's cheerleading team. The student's speech took place outside of school hours and away from the school's campus. In response, the school suspended the student for a year from the cheerleading team. We must decide whether [the] school's decision violated the First Amendment. Although we do not agree with the reasoning of the Third Circuit panel's majority, we do agree with its conclusion that the school's disciplinary action violated the First Amendment.

B. L. was a student at Mahanoy Area High School in Mahanoy City, Pennsylvania. At the end of her freshman year, B. L. tried out for a position on the school's varsity cheerleading squad. [She] did not make the varsity cheerleading team [but] was offered a spot on the cheerleading squad's junior varsity team. B. L. did not accept the coach's decision with good grace, particularly because the squad coaches had placed an entering freshman on the varsity team.

That weekend, B. L. and a friend visited [a] local convenience store. There, B. L. used her smartphone to post two photos on Snapchat, a social media application that allows users to post photos and videos that disappear after a set period of time. B. L. posted the images to her Snapchat "story," a feature of the application that allows any person in the user's "friend" group (B. L. had about 250 "friends") to view the images for a 24 hour period. The first image B. L. posted showed B. L. and a friend with middle fingers raised; it bore the caption: "Fuck school fuck softball fuck cheer fuck everything." The second image was blank but for a caption, which read: "Love how me and [another student] get told we need a year of jv before we make varsity but tha[t] doesn't matter to anyone else?" The caption also contained an upside-down smiley-face emoji.

B. L.'s Snapchat "friends" included other Mahanoy Area High School students, some of whom also belonged to the cheerleading squad. At least one of them, using a separate cellphone, took pictures of B. L.'s posts and shared them with other members of the cheerleading squad. One of the students who received these photos showed them to her mother (who was a cheerleading squad coach), and the images spread. That week, several cheerleaders and other students approached the cheerleading coaches "visibly upset" about B. L.'s posts. Questions about the posts persisted during an Algebra class taught by one of the two coaches. After discussing the matter with the school principal, the coaches decided that because the posts used profanity in connection with a school extracurricular activity, they violated team and school rules. As a result, the coaches suspended B. L. from the junior varsity cheerleading squad for the upcoming year. B. L.'s subsequent apologies did not move school officials. The school's athletic director, principal, superintendent, and school board all affirmed B. L.'s suspension from the team. In response, B. L., with her parents, filed this lawsuit in Federal District Court.

The District Court found in B. L.'s favor, [finding] that B. L.'s Snapchats had not caused substantial disruption at the school. [The] District Court declared that B. L.'s punishment violated the First Amendment, awarded B. L. nominal damages and attorneys' fees, and ordered the school to expunge her disciplinary record. On appeal, a panel of the Third Circuit affirmed. [The] majority noted that *Tinker* [held] that a public high school could not constitutionally prohibit a peaceful student political demonstration consisting of " 'pure speech' " on school property during the school day. In *Tinker*, this Court emphasized that there was no evidence the student protest would "substantially interfere with the work of the school or impinge upon the rights of other students." . . .

Many courts have taken this statement as setting a standard [that] allows schools considerable freedom on campus to discipline students for conduct that the First Amendment might otherwise protect. But here, the panel majority held that this additional freedom did "not apply to off-campus speech," which it defined as "speech that is outside school-owned, -operated, or -supervised channels and that is not reasonably interpreted as bearing the school's imprimatur." Because B. L.'s speech took place off campus, the panel concluded that [*Tinker*] did not apply and the school consequently could not discipline B. L. for engaging in a form of pure speech.

[We] have made clear that students do not "shed their constitutional rights to freedom of speech or expression," even "at the school house gate." But we have also made clear that courts must apply the First Amendment "in light of the special characteristics of the school environment." One such characteristic [is] that schools at times stand *in loco parentis*, *i.e.*, in the place of parents. This Court has [outlined] three specific categories of student speech that schools may regulate in certain circumstances: (1) "indecent," "lewd," or "vulgar" speech uttered during a school assembly on school grounds. *Bethel*. (2) speech, uttered during a class trip, that promotes "illegal drug use," *Morse* v. *Frederick*; and (3) speech that others may reasonably perceive as "bear[ing] the imprimatur of the school," [as] in a school-sponsored newspaper, *Kuhlmeier*. Finally, in *Tinker*, we said schools have a special interest in regulating speech that "materially disrupts classwork or involves substantial disorder or invasion of the rights of others."

Unlike the Third Circuit, we do not believe the special characteristics that give schools additional license to regulate student speech always disappear when a school regulates speech that takes place off campus. The school's regulatory interests remain significant in some off-campus circumstances. [These] include serious or severe bullying or harassment targeting particular individuals; threats aimed at teachers or other students; the failure to follow rules concerning lessons, the writing of papers, the use of computers, or participation in other online school activities; and breaches of school security devices, including material maintained within school computers.

Even B. L. herself and the *amici* supporting her would redefine the Third Circuit's off-campus/on-campus distinction, treating as on campus: all times when the school is responsible for the student; the school's immediate surroundings; travel en route to and from the school; all speech taking place over school laptops or on a school's website; speech taking place during remote learning; activities taken for school credit; and communications to school e-mail accounts or phones. And it may be that speech related to extracurricular activities, such as team sports, would also receive special treatment under B. L.'s proposed rule.

We are uncertain as to the length or content of any such list of appropriate exceptions or carveouts to the Third Circuit majority's rule. [Particularly] given the advent of computer-based learning, we hesitate to determine precisely which of many school-related off-campus activities belong on such a list. Neither do we now know how such a list might vary, depending upon a student's age, the nature of the school's off-campus activity, or the impact upon the school itself. Thus, we do not now set forth a broad, highly general First Amendment rule stating just what counts as "off campus" speech and whether or how ordinary First Amendment standards must give way off campus to a school's special need to prevent, *e.g.*, substantial disruption of learning-related activities or the protection of those who make up a school community.

We can, however, mention three features of off-campus speech that [distinguish] schools' efforts to regulate that speech from their efforts to regulate on-campus speech. [*First*,] a school, in relation to off-campus speech, will rarely stand *in loco parentis*. The doctrine of *in loco parentis* treats school administrators as standing in the place of students' parents under circumstances where the children's actual parents cannot protect, guide, and discipline them. Geographically speaking, off-campus speech will normally fall within the zone of parental, rather than school-related, responsibility. *Second*, from the student speaker's perspective, regulations of off-campus speech, when coupled with regulations of on-campus speech, include all the speech a student utters during the full 24-hour day. That means courts must be more skeptical of a school's efforts to regulate off-campus speech, for doing so may mean the student cannot engage in that kind of speech at all. When it comes to political or religious speech that occurs outside school or a school program or activity, the school will have a heavy burden to justify intervention. *Third*, the school itself has an interest in protecting a student's unpopular expression, especially when the expression takes place off campus. America's public schools are the nurseries of democracy. . . .

Given the many different kinds of off-campus speech, [we] can [say] little more than this: Taken together, these three features of much off-campus speech mean that the leeway the First Amendment grants to schools [is] diminished. We leave for future cases to decide where, when, and how these features mean the speaker's off-campus location will make the critical difference. This case can, however, provide one example. [Putting] aside the vulgar language, the listener would hear criticism of the team, the team's coaches, and the school—[i.e., criticism] of the rules of a community of which B. L. forms a part. This criticism did not involve features that place it outside the First Amendment's ordinary protection. B. L.'s posts, while crude, did not amount to fighting words. And while B. L. used vulgarity, her speech was not obscene as this Court has understood that term. To the contrary, B. L. uttered the kind of pure speech to which, were she an adult, the First Amendment would provide strong protection.

Consider too when, where, and how B. L. spoke. Her posts appeared outside of school hours from a location outside the school. She did not identify the school in her posts or target any member of the school community with vulgar or abusive language. B. L. also transmitted her speech through a personal cellphone, to an audience consisting of her private circle of Snapchat friends. These features of her speech, while risking transmission to the school itself, nonetheless diminish the school's interest in punishing B. L.'s utterance.

But what about the school's interest [in] prohibiting students from using vulgar language to criticize a school team or its coaches—at least when that criticism might well be transmitted to other students, team members, coaches, and faculty? We can break that general interest into three parts.

First, we consider the school's interest in teaching good manners and consequently in punishing the use of vulgar language aimed at part of the school community. The strength of this anti-vulgarity interest is weakened considerably by the fact that B. L. spoke outside the school on her own time. B. L. spoke under circumstances where the school did not stand *in loco parentis*. And there is no reason to believe B. L.'s parents had delegated to school officials their own control of B. L.'s behavior at the [convenience store]. Moreover, the vulgarity in B. L.'s posts encompassed a message, an expression of B. L.'s irritation with, and criticism of, the school and cheerleading communities. . . .

Second, the school argues that it was trying to prevent disruption [within] the bounds of a school-sponsored extracurricular activity. But we can find no evidence [of] the sort of "substantial disruption" of a school activity or a threatened harm to the rights of others that might justify the school's action. Rather, the record shows that discussion of the matter took, at most, 5 to 10 minutes of an Algebra class "for just a couple of days" and that some members of the cheerleading team were "upset" about the content of B. L.'s Snapchats. [As] we said in *Tinker,* "for the State in the person of school officials to justify prohibition of a particular expression of opinion, it must be able to show that its action was caused by something more than a mere desire to avoid the discomfort and unpleasantness that always accompany an unpopular viewpoint."

Third, the school presented some evidence that expresses [a] concern for team morale. There is [little,] however, that suggests any serious decline in team morale—to the point where it could create a substantial interference in, or disruption of, the school's efforts to maintain team cohesion. As we have said [in *Tinker,*] simple "undifferentiated fear or apprehension . . . is not enough to overcome the right to freedom of expression."

[Although] we do not agree with the reasoning of the Third Circuit majority, [we] agree that the school violated B. L.'s First Amendment rights. [Affirmed.]

JUSTICE ALITO, with whom JUSTICE GORSUCH joins, concurring.

I join the opinion of the Court but write separately to explain [the] framework within which I think cases like this should be analyzed. This is the first case in which we have considered [a] public school's attempt to regulate true off-premises student speech, and it is important that our opinion not be misunderstood.[2]

The Court holds—and I agree—that: the First Amendment permits public schools to regulate *some* student speech that does not occur on school premises during the regular school day. [I] also agree that it is not prudent for us to attempt at this time to "set forth a broad, highly general First Amendment rule" governing all off-premises speech. But [it] is helpful to

---

[2] [Ct's Note] This case does not involve speech by a student at a public college or university. For several reasons, including the age, independence, and living arrangements of such students, regulation of their speech may raise very different questions from those presented here. I do not understand the decision in this case to apply to such students.

consider the framework within which efforts to regulate off-premises speech should be analyzed.

[I] start with this threshold question: Why does the First Amendment ever allow the free-speech rights of public school students to be restricted to a greater extent than the rights of other juveniles who do not attend a public school? As the Court recognized in *Tinker*, when a public school regulates student speech, it acts as an arm of the State in which it is located. Suppose that B. L. had been enrolled in a private school and did exactly what she did in this case. [Pennsylvania] would have had no legal basis to punish her and almost certainly would not have even tried. So why should her status as a public school student give the Commonwealth any greater authority to punish her speech?

Our cases involving the regulation of student speech have not directly addressed this question. All those cases involved either in-school speech or speech that was tantamount to in-school speech. And in those cases, the Court appeared to take it for granted that "the special characteristics of the school environment" justified special rules. Why the Court took this for granted is not hard to imagine. As a practical matter, it is impossible to see how a school could function if administrators and teachers could not regulate on-premises student speech, including by imposing content-based restrictions in the classroom. In a math class, for example, the teacher can insist that students talk about math, not some other subject. In addition, when a teacher asks a question, the teacher must have the authority to insist that the student respond to that question and not some other question, and a teacher must also have the authority to speak without interruption and to demand that students refrain from interrupting one another. Practical necessity likewise dictates that teachers and school administrators have related authority with respect to other in-school activities like auditorium programs attended by a large audience. [But] when a public school regulates what students say or write when they are not on school grounds and are not participating in a school program, the school has the obligation to answer the question with which I began: Why should enrollment in a public school result in the diminution of a student's free-speech rights? The only plausible answer [is that] by enrolling a child in a public school, parents consent on behalf of the child to the relinquishment of some of the child's free-speech rights.

[When] it comes to children, courts [have] analyzed the issue of consent by adapting the common-law doctrine of *in loco parentis*. Under the common law, as Blackstone explained, "[a father could] delegate part of his parental authority . . . to the tutor or schoolmaster of his child; who is then *in loco parentis*, and has *such a portion of the power of the parent* committed to his charge, [namely,] that of restraint and correction, *as may be necessary to answer the purposes for which he is employed.*" [Today,] of course, the educational picture is quite different. [If] *in loco parentis* is transplanted [to] the 21st century United States, what it amounts to is simply a doctrine of inferred parental consent to a public school's exercise of a degree of authority that is commensurate with the task that the parents ask the school to perform. [So] how much authority to regulate speech do parents implicitly delegate when they enroll a child at a public school? The answer must be that parents are treated as having relinquished the measure of authority that the schools must be able to exercise in order to carry out their state-mandated educational mission, as well as the authority to perform any other functions to which parents expressly or implicitly agree—for example, by giving permission for a child to participate in an extracurricular activity or to go on a school trip.

I have already explained what this delegated authority means with respect to student speech during standard classroom instruction. And [this] authority extends to periods when students are in school but are not in class, for example, when they are walking in a hall, eating lunch, congregating outside before the school day starts, or waiting for a bus after school. [A] public school's regulation of off-premises student speech is a different matter. While the decision to enroll a student in a public school may be regarded as conferring the authority to regulate *some* off-premises speech, [enrollment] cannot be treated as a complete transfer of parental authority over a student's speech. [It] would be far-fetched to suggest that enrollment implicitly confers the right to regulate what a child says or writes at all times of day and throughout the calendar year.

[The] degree to which enrollment in a public school can be regarded as a delegation of authority over off-campus speech depends on the nature of the speech and the circumstances under which it occurs. [One] category of off-premises student speech falls easily within the scope of the authority that parents implicitly or explicitly provide. This category includes speech that takes place during or as part of what amounts to a temporal or spatial extension of the regular school program, *e.g.*, online instruction at home, assigned essays or other homework, and transportation to and from school. Also included are statements made during other school activities in which students participate with their parents' consent, such as school trips, school sports and other extracurricular activities that may take place after regular school hours or off school premises, and after-school programs for students who would otherwise be without adult supervision during that time. Abusive speech that occurs while students are walking to and from school may also fall into this category on the theory that it is school attendance that puts students on that route and in the company of the fellow students who engage in the abuse. The imperatives that justify the regulation of student speech while in school [apply] more or less equally to these off-premises activities.

[At] the other end of the spectrum, there is a category of speech that is almost always beyond the regulatory authority of a public school. This is student speech that is not expressly and specifically directed at the school, school administrators, teachers, or fellow students and that addresses matters of public concern, including sensitive subjects like politics, religion, and social relations. Speech on such matters lies at the heart of the First Amendment's protection, and the connection between student speech in this category and the ability of a public school to carry out its instructional program is tenuous. If a school tried to regulate such speech, the most that it could claim is that offensive off-premises speech on important matters may cause controversy and recriminations among students and may thus disrupt instruction and good order on school premises. But it is a "bedrock principle" that speech may not be suppressed simply because it expresses ideas that are "offensive or disagreeable."

[Between] these two extremes (*i.e.*, off-premises speech that is tantamount to on-campus speech and general statements made off premises on matters of public concern) lie the categories of off-premises student speech that appear to have given rise to the most litigation. A survey of lower court cases reveals several prominent categories. [One] group of cases involves perceived threats to school administrators, teachers, other staff members, or students. Laws that apply to everyone prohibit defined categories of threats. [Another] common category involves speech that criticizes or derides school administrators, teachers, or other staff members. Schools may assert that parents who send their children to a public school implicitly authorize the school to demand that the child exhibit the respect that is required for orderly and effective instruction, but parents surely do not relinquish their children's ability to complain in an appropriate manner about wrongdoing, dereliction, or even plain incompetence. Perhaps the most difficult category involves criticism or hurtful remarks about other students. Bullying and severe harassment are serious (and age-old) problems, but these concepts are not easy to define with the precision required for a regulation of speech.

The present case does not fall into any of these categories. Instead, it simply involves criticism (albeit in a crude manner) of the school and an extracurricular activity. Unflattering speech about a school or one of its programs is different from speech that criticizes or derides particular individuals, and [the] school's justifications for punishing B. L.'s speech were weak. [The] school did not claim that the messages caused any significant disruption of classes. [As] for the messages' effect on the morale of the cheerleading squad, the coach of a team sport may wish to take group cohesion and harmony into account in selecting members of the team, in assigning roles, and in allocating playing time, but it is self-evident that this authority has limits. [There] is, finally, the matter of B. L.'s language. There are parents who would not have been pleased with B. L.'s language and gesture, but whatever B. L.'s parents thought about what she did, it is not reasonable to infer that they gave the school the authority to regulate her choice of language when she was off school premises and not engaged in any school activity.

[The] overwhelming majority of school administrators, teachers, and coaches are men and women who are deeply dedicated to the best interests of their students, but it is predictable that there will be occasions when some will get carried away, as did the school officials in the case at hand. If today's decision teaches any lesson, it must be that the regulation of many types of off-premises student speech raises serious First Amendment concerns, and school officials should proceed cautiously before venturing into this territory.

JUSTICE THOMAS, dissenting.

B. L., a high school student, sent a profanity-laced message to hundreds of people, including classmates and team- mates. The message included a picture of B. L. raising her middle finger and captioned "F*** school" and "f*** cheer." This message was juxtaposed with another, which explained that B. L. was frustrated that she failed to make the varsity cheerleading squad. The cheerleading coach responded by disciplining B. L.

The Court overrides that decision—without even mentioning the 150 years of history supporting the coach. [When] students are on campus, the majority says, schools have authority *in loco parentis* [to] discipline speech and conduct. Off campus, the authority of schools is somewhat less. At that level of generality, I agree. But the majority omits important detail. What authority does a school have when it operates *in loco parentis*? How much less authority do schools have over off-campus speech and conduct? And how does a court decide if speech is on or off campus?

Disregarding these important issues, the majority simply posits three vague considerations and reaches an outcome. A more searching review reveals that schools historically could discipline students in circumstances like those presented here. Because the majority does not attempt to explain why we should not apply this historical rule and does not attempt to tether its approach to anything stable, I respectfully dissent.

[While] the majority entirely ignores the relevant history, I would begin the assessment of the scope of free-speech rights incorporated against the States by looking to "what 'ordinary citizens' at the time of [the Fourteenth Amendment's] ratification would have understood" the right to encompass. Cases and treatises from that era reveal that public schools retained substantial authority to discipline students: [A school could] regulate speech when it occurs off campus, so long as it has a proximate tendency to harm the school, its faculty or students, or its programs. [If] there is a good constitutional reason to depart from this historical rule, the majority and the parties fail to identify it.

[Our] modern doctrine is not to the contrary. "[T]he penalties imposed in this case were unrelated to any political viewpoint" or religious viewpoint. And although the majority sugar coats this speech as "criticism," it is well settled that schools can punish "vulgar" speech—at least when it occurs on campus. The discipline here—a 1-year suspension from the team—may strike some as disproportionate. But [there is] no textual or historical evidence to suggest that federal courts generally can police the proportionality of school disciplinary decisions in the name of the First Amendment.

The majority declines to consider [this] history, instead favoring a few pragmatic guideposts. [Consider] the Court's longtime failure to grapple with the historical doctrine of *in loco parentis*. [The] Fourteenth Amendment was ratified against the background legal principle that publicly funded schools operated [as] delegated substitutes of parents. This principle freed schools from the constraints the Fourteenth Amendment placed on other government actors. [Plausible] arguments can be raised in favor of departing from that historical doctrine. When the Fourteenth Amendment was ratified, just three jurisdictions had compulsory-education laws. One might argue that [*in*] *loco parentis* applies only when delegation is voluntary. The Court, however, did not make that (or any other) argument against this historical doctrine. [It] acknowledges that schools act *in loco parentis* when students speak on campus [but] fails to address the historical contours of that doctrine, whether the doctrine applies to off-campus speech, or why the Court has abandoned it. [Moreover,] the majority uncritically adopts the assumption that B. L.'s speech, in fact, was off campus. But the location of her speech is a much trickier question than the majority acknowledges. Because speech travels, schools sometimes may be able to treat speech as on campus even though it originates off campus. Nobody doubts, for example, that a school . . . can discipline [a student] when he passes out vulgar flyers on campus—even if he creates those flyers off campus. The same may be true in many contexts when social media speech is generated off campus but received on campus. [Here,] it makes sense to treat B. L.'s speech as off-campus speech. There is little evidence that B. L.'s speech was received on campus. [But] the majority mentions none of this. It simply, and uncritically, assumes that B. L.'s speech was off campus. . . .

[The] Court transparently takes a common-law approach to today's decision. It states just one rule: Schools can regulate speech less often when that speech occurs off campus. It then identifies this case as an "example" and "leav[es] for future cases" the job of developing this new common-law doctrine. But the Court's foundation is untethered from anything stable, and courts (and schools) will almost certainly be at a loss as to what exactly the Court's opinion today means. [Because] it reaches the wrong result under the appropriate historical test, I respectfully dissent.

9. THE RIGHT NOT TO SPEAK, THE RIGHT TO ASSOCIATE, AND THE RIGHT NOT TO ASSOCIATE

I. THE RIGHT NOT TO BE ASSOCIATED WITH PARTICULAR IDEAS

P. 1162, add as new note 10 after note 9:

10. *Compelled disclosures revisited.* Both *NAACP v. Alabama, supra,* and *Shelton v. Tucker,* 364 U.S. 479 (1960), dealt with Civil Rights era attempts to intimidate civil rights organization by requiring disclosure of membership lists. In *Americans for Prosperity Foundation v. Bonta,* 141 S.Ct. 2373 (2021), the Court revisited that issue and seemed to extend and strengthen that aspect of the freedom of association, even outside of the civil rights context and even absent evidence of the kind of actual or potential intimidation that was at issue in *NAACP* and *Shelton.*

At issue in *Americans for Prosperity* was a challenge to a California Attorney General's regulation, adopted and administered pursuant to the Attorney General's statutory authority to regulate charitable organizations, requiring that regulated charities disclose their major donors, typically those whose donations were $5000 per year or more. Two charitable organizations, one (Americans for Prosperity) with a focus on economic liberty and related issues, and the other (Thomas More Law Center) focused substantially on issues of religious freedom, challenged the donor disclosure requirement, and the Court, per ROBERTS, C.J., upheld the challenge, relying on *NAACP* and *Shelton* and finding the restriction to be an unjustified restriction on the First Amendment's implicit protection of freedom of expression.

Four issues dominated the various opinions. One was the level of scrutiny. Neither *NAACP* nor *Shelton* had specified the appropriate level of scrutiny for compelled membership or donor disclosures, but the Court in *Buckley v. Valeo* (1976, sec. 10, *infra*) had held that required disclosures in the campaign finance context must be measured under a standard of "exacting scrutiny." And although one of the challenging organizations had argued that exacting scrutiny was the equivalent of strict scrutiny, with the latter's requirement of "the least restrictive alternative," the Court in *Americans for Prosperity* held that exacting scrutiny was as applicable outside of the campaign and election context as within it, and that it required both a "sufficiently important governmental interest" and means of pursuing that interest that were "narrowly tailored," although not the least restrictive alternative. "Where exacting scrutiny applies, the challenged requirement must be narrowly tailored to the interest it promotes, even if it is not the least restrictive means of achieving that end."

Reversing the Ninth Circuit, the Court found California's interest in "preventing wrongdoing by charitable organizations" sufficiently important, but concluded that the disclosure requirement was not narrowly tailored to achieve that end. "In reality, then, California's interest is less in investigating fraud and more in ease of administration. . . . But [mere] administrative convenience does not remotely 'reflect the seriousness of the actual burden.' *Doe v. Reed*, 561 U.S. 186 (2010)."

The second issue was the existence or not of an actual threat of actual donor intimidation. Finding the possibility of actual intimidation remote and speculative, SOTOMAYOR, J., joined by Breyer and Kagan, JJ, dissenting, insisted that this case differed substantially from both *NAACP* and *Shelton*, where there had been actual evidence of genuinely threatened intimidation: "[Not] all reporting and disclosure regimes burden associational rights in the same way. [Regardless] of whether there is any risk of public disclosure, and no matter if the burdens on associational rights are slight, heavy, or non-existent, disclosure regimes must [now] be narrowly tailored. The Court searches in vain to find a foothold for this new approach. . . . [Today's] decision discards decades of First Amendment jurisprudence recognizing that reporting and disclosure requirements do not directly burden associational rights."

The third issue was whether the alleged defects in California's approach justified a facial challenge and thus facial invalidation. Under the majority's approach, which it labeled an application of First Amendment overbreadth doctrine, "the lack of tailoring to the State's investigative goal is categorical—present in every case—as is the weakness of the State's interest in administrative convenience. Every demand that might chill association therefore fails exacting scrutiny." And although Justice Sotomayor's dissent implied that she might not even have found intimidation or chilling with respect to these particular challengers, she argued more strongly that the case was inappropriate for facial invalidation: "If the Court had simply granted as-applied relief to petitioners based on its reading of the facts [and the fear of reprisals by these donors], I would be sympathetic, although my own views diverge. [But] the Court jettisons completely the longstanding requirement that plaintiffs demonstrate an actual burden [to them] before the Court will subject governmental action to close scrutiny. It then invalidates a regulation in its entirety, even though it can point to no record evidence demonstrating that the regulation is likely to chill a substantial proportion of donors."[1]

---

[1]   Thomas, J., joining the majority in all except its decision to characterize the case as a facial challenge, objected once again to the Court's overbreadth doctrine, and objected to characterizing it as either an overbreadth claim or a facial challenge: "The Court simply (and correctly) holds that the District Court properly enjoined the law *as applied* to petitioners." "A declaration that the law is 'facially' unconstitutional' seems to me no more than an advisory opinion—which a federal court should never issue at all." Alito, J., joined by Gorsuch, J., also joined all of the majority opinion except for its discussion of the distinction between exacting and strict scrutiny, seeing "no need to decide [now] which standard should be applied here or whether the same level of scrutiny should apply in all [compelled disclosure] cases."

10. WEALTH, EQUALITY, AND THE POLITICAL PROCESS

P. 1179, add as new paragraph at end of footnote 305:

Do disclosure requirements, even without limitations on the amounts, create First Amendment problems in campaign finance context? The issue lurked around *Americans for Prosperity Foundation v. Bonta*, 141 S.Ct. 2373 (2021), discussed above, addition to p. 1162.

CHAPTER 8

FREEDOM OF RELIGION

■ ■ ■

1. THE ESTABLISHMENT CLAUSE

IV. OFFICIAL ACKNOWLEDGMENT OF RELIGION

P. 1270, at the end of note 1:

AMERICAN LEGION v. AMERICAN HUMANIST ASS'N, 139 S.Ct. 2067 (2019), again addressed the issue of public monuments with religious origins and connotations. At issue was the so-called Peace Cross in Bladensburg, Maryland. The cross was planned in 1918 as a memorial to the forty-nine Prince George's County solders who had been killed during the First World War. Finally constructed in 1925, the cross was a 32-foot tall "plain Latin cross" on a stone pedestal located on a traffic island at one end of one of the major highways connecting Washington, D.C., with Annapolis, Maryland. The cross, located on state-owned land and maintained by a state agency, was challenged as a violation of the Establishment Clause, but the Court, in a complex series of opinions, rejected the challenge, and in the process put what appears to be virtually the final nail in the coffin of the *Lemon* test.

ALITO, J., in an opinion that was mostly the opinion of the Court, noted that the *Lemon* test was especially unsuitable for "cases . . . that involve the use, for ceremonial, celebratory, or commemorative purposes, of words or symbols with religious associations," and that there should be a "presumption of constitutionality for longstanding monuments, symbols, and practices." More particularly, and as in *Salazar v. Buono*, infra, "[many] years after the fact . . . [there is] no way to be certain about the motivations of the men who were responsible for the creation of the monument." And as in *Van Orden*, *supra*, and *McCreary*, *supra*, "the purposes associated with an established monument, symbol, or practice often multiply." Moreover, "just as the purpose for maintaining a monument, symbol, or practice may evolve," so too may the message it conveys. And as a result, he said, the very act of removal may be understood as "aggressively hostile to removal."

Applying these concerns to the case at hand, Alito documented the way in which crosses in general, and not just this cross, had come to represent memorials to soldiers and to bravery. This was similar, he said, to the names of places, and "few would say that the State of California is attempting to convey a religious message by retaining the names given . . . by [the] original Spanish settlers [to] San Diego, Los Angeles, Santa Barbara, San Jose, San

Francisco, etc." "The cross is undoubtedly a Christian symbol, but that fact should not blind us to everything else that the Bladensburg Cross has come to represent. For some, that monument is a symbolic resting place for ancestors who never returned home. For others, it is a place for the community to gather and honor all veterans and their sacrifices for our Nation. For others still, it is a historical landmark. For many of these people, destroying [the] Cross that has stood undisturbed for nearly a century would not be neutral and would not further the ideals of respect and tolerance embodied in the First Amendment. [This] Cross does not offend the Constitution."

BREYER, J., joined by Kagan, J., concurred, observing that different considerations might apply to newer monuments in different contexts. KAVANAUGH, J., also concurred, explicitly emphasizing the way in which the *Lemon* test could not explain the Court's Establishment Clause jurisprudence for the 48 years since it was decided. But KAGAN, J., also concurring with most of Alito's opinion, remained of the belief that although "the *Lemon* test does not solve every Establishment Clause problem, [its] focus on purposes and effects [remains] crucial in evaluating government action in this sphere." THOMAS, J., concurring in the judgment, and describing the *Lemon* test as "long-discredited," reiterated his longstanding resistance to the incorporation of the Establishment Clause and thus its application to the states. "And even if [the Establishment Clause did apply to the states,] this religious display does not involve the type of actual legal coercion that was a hallmark of historical establishments of religion." GORSUCH, J., in an opinion joined by Thomas, J., concurred only in the judgment, insisting that merely being offended by the memorial's presence—"offended observer standing"—was insufficient to confer standing to sue in the first place, but also describing *Lemon* as a "misadventure." GINSBURG, J., joined by Sotomayor, J., dissented, documenting that most war memorials, including most of the World War I memorials, do not contain crosses or other religious symbols, and arguing that "[j]ust as a Star of David is not suitable to honor Christians who died serving their country, so is a cross not suitable to honor those of other faiths who died defending their nation. [By] maintaining the Peace Cross on a public highway, [Maryland] elevates Christianity over other faiths, and religion over nonreligion. [When] a cross is displayed on public property, the government may be presumed to endorse its religious content."

2. THE FREE EXERCISE CLAUSE AND RELATED STATUTORY ISSUES

I. CONFLICT WITH STATE REGULATION

P. 1299, at end of footnote 94, insert the following as new paragraph:

Litigation regarding the contraceptive mandate of the Affordable Care Act has continued, with the issue of religious exemptions to the mandate raising numerous statutory issues. In *Little Sisters of the Poor Saints Peter and Paul Home v. Pennsylvania*, 140 S.Ct. 2367 (2020), a Supreme Court majority reversed a Third Circuit ruling and upheld the statutory authority of the

Departments of Health and Human Services, Labor, and Treasury to create exemptions from the contraceptive mandate for employers with religious or moral objections to the mandate's requirements. Writing for the majority, Thomas, J., noted that no constitutional question had been raised in the litigation, and concluded that the plain language of the Affordable Care Act authorized all three departments to create the religious and moral exemptions. In a concurring opinion, Alito, J., joined by Gorsuch, J., argued that the religious exemption was required by the Religious Freedom Restoration Act, and thus would be necessary even apart from the language of the Affordable Care Act. Kagan, J., joined by Breyer, J., concurred only in the judgment, and emphasized that on remand the exemption would have to be measured against the administrative law requirement of "reasoned decisionmaking," and hinted that the exemption in its existing form might not satisfy this requirement. Ginsburg, J., joined by Sotomayor, J., dissented, arguing that the Women's Health Amendment to the Affordable Care Act required that contraceptive services be made available even in the face of a claimed exemption by employers.

P. 1305, at the end of note 2:

Trinity Lutheran, in being about funding for the resurfacing of a religious school's playground, appeared to involve only state support for the non-religious activities of a religious institution. Whether the decision would also permit funding by a government program of general application for those parts of a religious institution that were more closely related to the institution's religious mission remained an open question. That question became less open, however, after the Court's 2020 decision in ESPINOZA v. MONTANA DEPARTMENT OF REVENUE, 140 S.Ct. 2246 (2020).

At issue in *Espinoza* was a Montana program providing a $150 tax credit to those who made donations to organizations awarding scholarships for private school tuition. Under the Montana program, the tax credit was available without regard to whether the private schools that were supported (by the choice of the scholarship recipients) were religious or secular. Although a program allowing such indirect support for religious schools would not, under existing doctrine, run afoul of the Establishment Clause (*Locke*; *Trinity Lutheran*), both the Montana Department of Revenue and then the Montana Supreme Court concluded that the program nevertheless violated the "no aid" provision of the Montana Constitution, a provision prohibiting "direct or indirect" public funding of any school, college, or university "controlled in whole or in part by any church, sect, or denomination." The issue before the Court in *Espinoza* was whether excluding religious schools from benefiting from an indirect funding program of general application, as the Montana Supreme Court concluded that the Montana Constitution required, violated the Free Exercise Clause of the First Amendment.

Writing for a 5–4 majority, ROBERTS, C.J., held that Montana's exclusion of schools operated by religious organizations from an otherwise comprehensive program of support for private schools violated the Free Exercise Clause. Relying heavily on *Trinity Lutheran*, the majority concluded that "disqualifying otherwise eligible recipients from a public benefit 'solely because of their religious character' triggered strict Free Exercise scrutiny, and that Montana had not demonstrated that the exclusion served interests "of the highest order" (*Lukumi*) and was "narrowly tailored in pursuit of those interests."

Unlike *Locke*, which involved support for the training of clergy, there was no indication in *Espinoza* that the indirect funding would necessarily wind up supporting explicitly religious activities. But the Court found such a distinction unavailing, and indeed irrelevant, concluding that strict Free Exercise scrutiny was triggered by discrimination based on the religious *status* of an institution, without regard to whether the supported activities—the *use* of the funds—were or were not religious in character.

THOMAS, J., joined by Gorsuch, J., concurred with the majority opinion, but wrote separately to reiterate his view that the Fourteenth Amendment did not incorporate the Establishment Clause. For Justice Thomas, the Establishment Clause was too-often employed to validate what would otherwise be Free Exercise violations, and "unincorporating" the Establishment Clause would remove a frequent obstacle to full realization of Free Exercise values.

ALITO, J., also issued a concurring opinion, detailing the way in which Montana's "no aid" constitutional provision, like those in thirty-eight other states, was modeled after the ultimately unsuccessful attempts in the "Blaine Amendment" proposal of 1876 to amend the United States Constitution. The Blaine Amendment movement, Justice Alito argued, was based on explicitly anti-Catholic sentiments, sentiments arising out of anti-immigrant feelings that were pervasive at the time. This history, Justice Alito suggested, provided the context in which Montana's actions should be viewed, a context highlighting the anti-religious motivations that should even now inform the understanding of "sectarian" in provisions such as that in the Montana Constitution. And GORSUCH, J.'s separate concurring opinion focused on the status/use distinction, arguing that "[t]he right to *be* religious without the right to *do* religious things would hardly amount to a right at all."

GINSBURG, J., joined by Kagan, J., dissented, emphasizing the fact that the Montana Supreme Court had, because it believed that the scholarship program violated the Montana Constitution's no-aid provision, invalidated the entire program. For Justice Ginsburg, this meant that there was no program in place, thus eliminating any possibility of discrimination between secular and sectarian schools. Under the Montana Supreme Court's ruling, she insisted, no one received anything, and thus there could be no claim that secular institutions were receiving benefits or support that sectarian institutions were not. [In his majority opinion, Chief Justice Roberts addressed this argument, maintaining that the Montana Supreme Court's invalidation of the entire program was based on a misreading of *federal* constitutional law, a misreading that the Supreme Court was empowered to correct.]

BREYER, J., also dissented, joined in part by Kagan, J. He objected to an "overly rigid" application of the combination of the Establishment and Free Exercise Clauses, urging the majority to be faithful to the "play-in-the-joints" idea suggested in *Trinity Lutheran*. Applying this more flexible and context-specific approach, Breyer took issue with the majority's focus on the status of the recipient institutions and argued that what should matter was what the institution would *do* with the support. And he saw the Montana situation as one in which the recipient institutions, as in *Locke*, would be using state support "for the inculcation of religious truths" precisely because "religious schools seek generally to inspire religious faith and values in their students."

SOTOMAYOR, J., dissented as well, agreeing with Justice Ginsburg that, with no program in force, there was no extant discrimination and thus no case to decide. And Justice Sotomayor also reprised her dissent in *Trinity Lutheran*, seeing the Montana Supreme Court's decision as amounting to little more than a refusal by the state to "pay for [a] religious practice," a refusal that did not violate the Free Exercise Clause.

P. 1306, at end of note 4, insert the following as new paragraph:

The scope of the so-called ministerial exemption from much of state and federal employment law was expanded at the end of the 2019 Term in *Our Lady of Guadalupe School v. Morrissey-Berru*, 140 S.Ct. 2049 (2020). Although the teacher in *Hosanna-Tabor* had been formally designated by her religious school employer as a "minister," and although she had received considerable religious training, the Court in *Our Lady of Guadalupe* held that neither of these attributes were necessary for the application of the ministerial exemption. Writing for a 7–2 majority, Alito, J., emphasized that the criteria set forth in *Hosanna-Tabor* were not to be understood as a rigid formula, and that the teachers whose employment was at issue in the two consolidated cases had substantial responsibilities for religious education in their respective religious schools. Even though neither was designated as a minister, even though both had been trained in the liberal arts and not in religion, and even though both were involved in teaching non-religious subjects, their actual job duties included a sufficient amount of religious instruction and inculcation to qualify them for the ministerial exemption. Thomas, J., joined by Gorsuch, J., concurred in the Court's judgment and opinion, but wrote separately to emphasize that the religion clauses did not permit the courts to second-guess the good-faith determination by a religious institution of who did or did not qualify as a minister. Sotomayor, J., joined by Ginsburg, J., dissented, charging the majority with having distorted the facts, with granting undue deference to a religious institution's determination of the nature of the employee's responsibilities, and of being insufficiently attentive to the basic principle of *Employment Division v. Smith*, *supra*, that "religious entities" must "abide by generally applicable laws," especially laws dealing with discrimination in employment.

P. 1307, as new note after note 5:

6. ***Smith under attack.*** *Employment Division v. Smith*'s basic principle—that the effect on religious practices of regulatory laws of general application that neither single out religion nor result from religious animus will not produce substantially heightened scrutiny—remains standing but continues to be the subject of frontal challenge. *Lukumi* and *Masterpiece Cakeshop* avoided the challenge by finding evidence of hostility to religion, and

the Court once again declined to take on *Smith* directly in FULTON v. CITY OF PHILADELPHIA, 141 S.Ct 1868 (2021). At issue in *Fulton* was an arrangement in which Philadelphia contracted with various non-governmental agencies to manage the placement of children with foster families. One of those agencies was Catholic Social Services (CSS), which refused to certify same-sex couples to be foster parents because of CSS's religious beliefs in opposition to same-sex marriage. The City, after an investigation, informed CSS that it would no longer continue the same arrangement as had existed in the past unless CSS agreed to certify same-sex married couples as foster parents on the same terms as it certified opposite-sex married couples. CSS challenged the city's actions as burdening their religious practices and beliefs and as discriminating against CSS because of its religious beliefs, all in violation of the Free Exercise Clause. And although the Court upheld CSS's challenge, it did so without confronting the basic holding of *Employment Division v. Smith*. Rather, the Court unanimously concluded that the City's selective and discretionary method of choosing agencies with which to contract for foster parent placement removed the City's actions from *Smith*'s category of actions and regulations of general applicability. Because the discretionary aspect of choosing foster placement agencies made *Smith* inapplicable, *Smith*'s minimal scrutiny for burdens on religion incidental to laws of general application was not, the Court held, at issue.

Writing for the Court, ROBERTS, C.J., concluded that excluding CSS from the City's foster placement program, being discretionary and not the byproduct of a law or regulation of general applicability, must be examined and evaluated under a "strict scrutiny" standard of review. "[Because the City's] non-discrimination requirement imposes a burden on CSS's religious exercise and does not qualify as generally applicable," those actions "are subject to 'the most rigorous of scrutiny' *Lukumi*." "Because the City's actions are therefore examined under the strictest scrutiny regardless of *Smith*, we have no occasion to reconsider that decision here."

As in *Masterpiece Cakeshop*, Philadelphia argued that a broad and generally applicable anti-discrimination law—here, the Philadelphia Fair Practices Ordinance—made the situation at issue in *Fulton* comparable to that in *Smith*. But the Fair Practices Ordinance applied only to places of "public accommodation," and the Chief Justice's opinion rejected the view that services provided by CSS counted as a public accommodation for purposes of determining the constitutional question whether this was a law of general application in the relevant sense. As a result, the only relevant legal provision remaining was that section of the "standard foster care contract" that allowed the Commissioner of the Department of Human Services to grant exceptions "in his/her sole discretion" to its requirement that providers not reject prospective foster parents because of their sexual orientation. This power to grant exceptions, the Chief Justice concluded, fell squarely within *Smith*'s conclusion that a law was not generally applicable "if it 'invite[s]' the government to consider the particular reasons for a person's conduct by providing 'a mechanism for individualized exceptions' " (*Smith*, quoting the opinion of Burger, C.J., in *Bowen v. Roy,* 476 U.S. 693, 708 (1986). And Chief Justice Roberts went on to observe that *Sherbert v. Verner,* 374 U.S. 398 (1963), relied upon by Philadelphia, had also been decided on the same grounds of lack of general applicability by virtue of the availability of individually-assessed exemptions.

Smith having been deemed inapplicable, the Court had little difficulty in applying strict scrutiny and finding Philadelphia's justifications for excluding CSS unavailing. "[T]he City's asserted interests are insufficient. Maximizing the number of foster families and minimizing liability are important goals, but the City fails to show that granting CSS an exception will put those goals at risk. [That] leaves the interest of the City in the equal treatment of prospective foster parents and foster children. We do not doubt that this interest is a weighty one, for '[o]ur society has come to the recognition that gay persons and gay couples cannot be treated as social outcasts or as inferior in dignity and worth.' *Masterpiece Cakeshop.* On the facts of this case, however, this interest cannot justify denying CSS an exception for its religious exercise. The creation of a system of exceptions under the contract undermines the City's contention that its non-discrimination policies can brook no departures."

Justice Barrett, joined by Justice Kavanaugh, issued a concurring opinion joining the majority opinion "in full." But she observed that she found the arguments against *Smith* "more compelling," seeing no reason to treat the Free Exercise Clause as "offer[ing] nothing more than protection from discrimination." And although Justice Breyer did not join this part of Justice Barrett's opinion, he did join the remainder of her opinion, in which she expressed uncertainty about what might replace *Smith* and agreed that this was not the case to decide "whether *Smith* should be overruled, much less what should replace it."

Justice Alito, joined by Justices Thomas and Gorsuch, concurred only in the judgment, arguing that that the Court's reasons for refusing to consider directly the status of *Smith* were flimsy, and that, in actual practice, the Philadelphia arrangements were indeed the kind of laws of general application to which *Smith* applied. He then went on to argue directly against *Smith,* insisting that it represented a departure from *Sherbert v. Verner, Wisconsin v. Yoder, Hobbie v. Unemployment Appeals Commission,* among others, and that both the history and the constitutional text demanded that the Free Exercise Clause be interpreted in a "straightforward" manner to prohibit the "forbidding or hindering unrestrained religious practices or worship." This interpretation, Justice Alito argued, makes the Free Exercise Clause more than a mere non-discrimination provision, and he claimed that it is an interpretation of the Free Exercise Clause supported by the historical record, a record that Justice Alito set forth in great depth and detail. He also discussed at length the way other provisions of the Bill of Rights had been interpreted to require more than non-discrimination, including, for example, the Sixth Amendment's guarantee of a right to counsel. Were *Smith* to be overruled, Justice Alito argued, it could be replaced with the standard he believed *Smith* replaced: "A law that imposes a substantial burden on religious exercise can be sustained only if it is narrowly tailored to serve a compelling government interest." And he pointed to both the Religious Freedom Restoration Act (RFRA) and the Religious Land Use and Institutionalized Persons Act (RLUIPA) as demonstrating that his proposed test, one similar to that imposed by these statutes, would be both workable and interpretable.

Justice Gorsuch, although joining Justice Alito's opinion, also filed his own opinion concurring in the judgment, an opinion joined by Justices Thomas and Alito. Justice Gorsuch also objected to the Court's refusal to take on *Smith* directly. "To be sure, any time this Court turns from misguided precedent back toward the Constitution's original public meaning, challenging questions may arise across a large field of cases and controversies. But that's no excuse for refusing to apply the original public meaning in the dispute actually before us. Rather than adhere to *Smith* until we settle on some 'grand unified theory' of the Free Exercise Clause for all future cases until the end of time, the Court should overrule it now, set us back on the correct course, and address each case as it comes."

If and when (with when being more likely than if) the Court directly address's *Smith*'s vitality and its underlying question of what counts as a law of general application, two recent per curiam decisions on the application of COVID-19 restrictions to religious gatherings appear to signal both the issues and the Court's possible resolution of them. Both SOUTH BAY PENTECOSTAL CHURCH v. NEWSOM, 2021 WL 2250818 (2021) and TANDON v. NEWSOM, 141 S.Ct. 1294 (2021) were per curiam decisions dealing with California's COVID-19 restrictions on gatherings as those restrictions applied to religious services and other religious gatherings. In *South Bay*, the Court, with a complex series of opinions, enjoined by per curiam order California's prohibition on indoor worship services but refused to enjoin the capacity restriction and the restriction on singing and chanting. Justice Gorsuch, joined by Justices Alito and Thomas, would have enjoined all of the restrictions on Free Exercise grounds, and Justice Kagan, dissenting and joined by Justices Breyer and Sotomayor, would have enjoined none of them, believing that California had presented ample scientific evidence in support of its restrictions.

The larger Free Exercise issues were presented more clearly in *Tandon*, which reversed the Ninth Circuit's refusal to enjoin enforcement of California's restriction on household religious gatherings to three households. Because the same restriction also restricted some but not all non-religious household gatherings in the same way, the question was whether the existence of a restriction imposed on the exercise of religion could be considered neutral if it was also imposed on some similar non-religious activities, or if instead the very fact that some nonreligious activities were not so restricted made the regulation a neutral one. Does the existence of similarly regulated secular activity make a restriction on religious activity neutral and general, as the Ninth Circuit concluded, or does the fact that at least *some* secular activities are treated differently from religious activities suffice to make the restriction non-neutral? In other words, what is the relevant comparison group or activity for determining neutrality and generality?

In *Tandon*'s per curiam opinion, the Court rejected the Ninth Circuit's view, concluding that differential treatment between religious activity and some secular activity made the restriction non-neutral, even when there were some secular activities that were treated the same as the religious activities. And so although the California law imposed its three-household limit on many non-religious gatherings as well as on religious gatherings, the Court concluded that the existence of secular activities—many of them commercial—that were not restricted but otherwise similar to the religious activities was sufficient to defeat the claim of neutrality, meaning that strict scrutiny would be applied to the restriction.

Chief Justice Roberts did not join the Court's ruling, believing that injunctive relief was inappropriate at this stage of the proceedings. And Justice Kagan, dissenting and joined by Justices Breyer and Sotomayor, argued that the Court had ignored the empirical evidence that California had offered, evidence supporting its view that the non-regulated secular activities were less of a risk for COVID-19 transmission than the regulated religious and secular activities. For example, she argued, California had offered evidence to support the view that duration of exposure was a COVID-19 transmission risk factor and that religious gatherings involved lengthier time together than, for example, many commercial gatherings and transactions. And thus although the majority and the dissenters agreed in theory that neutrality could be defeated by treating relevantly similar religious and non-religious activities differently, the question here, and one likely to recur, and especially if *Smith* remains controlling, is what is to count as relevantly similar.

CHAPTER 9

EQUAL PROTECTION

■ ■ ■

2. RACE AND ETHNIC ANCESTRY

IV. DE JURE VS. DE FACTO DISCRIMINATION

P. 1454, after *Abbott v. Perez*:

———

In DEPARTMENT OF HOMELAND SECURITY v. REGENTS OF UNIVERSITY OF CALIFORNIA, 140 S.Ct. 1891 (2020), the Court, per ROBERTS, C.J., held that the Department of Homeland Security violated the Administrative Procedure Act (by failing to provide an adequately reasoned explanation for its decision) when it rescinded an order allowing unauthorized aliens who arrived in the United States as children to apply for temporary suspension of removal. At the same time, the Court held that the challengers had not adequately pleaded a claim that the agency acted for racially discriminatory reasons. The plaintiffs had cited no evidence of discriminatory motive by the immediately responsible officials—the Attorney General and the Acting Secretary of the Department of Homeland Security—and statements by President Trump that allegedly manifest hostility to Latinos were "remote in time and made in unrelated contexts." Sotomayor, J., dissented on the equal protection question: "[T]he impact of the policy decision must be viewed in the context of the President's public statements on and off the campaign trail."

4. SPECIAL SCRUTINY FOR OTHER CLASSIFICATIONS: DOCTRINE AND DEBATES

I. SEXUAL ORIENTATION

P. 1545, at the end of note 3:

In *Bostock v. Clayton County*, 140 S.Ct. 1731 (2020), the Court, per Gorsuch, J., held by 6–3 that an employer's firing of an employee "simply for being homosexual or transgender" constitutes forbidden discrimination on the basis of "sex" under Title VII of the 1964 Civil Rights Act: "Consider, for example, an employer with two employees, both of whom are attracted to men. The two individuals are, to the employer's mind, materially identical in all respects, except that one is a man and the other a woman. If the employer fires the male employee for no reason other than the fact he is attracted to men, the employer discriminates against him for traits or actions it tolerates in his female colleague . . . . It doesn't matter if other factors besides the plaintiff's sex contributed to the decision."

Alito, J., joined by Thomas, J., dissented, as did Kavanaugh, J. The dissenting opinions stressed that "sex discrimination" and discrimination based on LGBT status are different concepts that reflect different attitudes and motivations. Alito, J., thought it among *Bostock*'s likely consequences that "despite the important differences between the Fourteenth Amendment and Title VII, the Court's decision may exert a gravitational pull" toward subjecting anti-LGBT discrimination to the same elevated scrutiny as sex discrimination in suits alleging constitutional violations.

5. FUNDAMENTAL RIGHTS

I. VOTING

D. "Dilution" of the Right: Partisan Gerrymanders

P. 1608, after the first full paragraph, substitute the following paragraph for *Davis v. Bandemer*, *Vieth v. Jubelirer*, and the Notes and Questions that follow on pp. 1616–19:

In DAVIS v. BANDEMER, 478 U.S. 109 (1986), the Court divided over the test to apply to identify constitutionally forbidden partisan gerrymanders under the Equal Protection Clause. WHITE, J., joined by Brennan, Marshall, and Blackmun, JJ., would have required proof of "intentional discrimination against an identifiable political group and an actual discriminatory effect on that group." POWELL, J., joined by Stevens, J., would have focused on "whether the boundaries of the voting districts have been distorted deliberately and arbitrarily to achieve illegitimate ends." A dissenting opinion, by O'CONNOR, J., joined by Burger, C.J., and Rehnquist, J., would have held that challenges to partisan gerrymanders pose nonjusticiable political questions because the Equal Protection Clause simply "does not supply judicially manageable standards for resolving" them.

The view that challenges to partisan gerrymanders present political questions, which gained the support of a plurality of the Justices in *Vieth v. Jubelier*, 541 U.S. 267 (2004), prevailed, by a vote of 5 to 4, in *Rucho v. Common Cause*, p. 1 of this Supplement. *Rucho*, which you should re-read at this time, states the governing law on the constitutional permissibility of partisan gerrymanders. As you re-read Roberts, C.J.'s, majority opinion, consider what practical difference there is, if any, between its ruling that challengers to political gerrymanders pose nonjusticiable political questions and an "on the merits" conclusion that partisan gerrymanders do not violate the Equal Protection Clause or any other provision of the Constitution.

CHAPTER 10

THE CONCEPT OF STATE ACTION

■ ■ ■

2. "GOVERNMENT FUNCTION"

III. REFUSALS TO FIND "GOVERNMENTAL FUNCTION"

P. 1674, after *Jackson v. Metropolitan Edison Co.*:

———

MANHATTAN COMMUNITY ACCESS CORP. v. HALLECK, 139 S.Ct. 1921 (2019), held that a private entity administering the public access channels on a New York cable system was not a state actor despite having been designated to perform that function by the City of New York. New York state law "requires cable operators in the State to set aside channels on their cable systems for public access" and further "requires that use of the public access channels be free of charge and first-come, first-served. Under state law, the cable operator operates the public access channels unless the local government in the area chooses to itself operate the channels or designates a private entity to operate the channels." For the Time-Warner cable system in Manhattan, New York City designated a private nonprofit corporation, Manhattan Neighborhood Network (MNN), to operate the legally mandated public access channels. After the respondents produced a film critical of MNN and MNN televised it, MNN suspended the respondents from further access to MNN facilities. Respondents then sued, alleging that the public access channels were a public forum and that MNN's actions violated their First Amendment rights.

Per KAVANAUGH, J., the Court, by 5–4, ordered dismissal on the ground that MNN is not a state actor. Although "a private entity may qualify as a state actor when it exercises 'powers traditionally exclusively reserved to the State,' " *Jackson v. Metropolitan Edison Co.*, the function of operating "public access channels on a cable system [h]as not traditionally and exclusively been performed by government. Since the 1970s, when public access channels became a regular feature on cable systems, a variety of private and public actors have operated public access channels, including: private cable operators; private nonprofit organizations;

75

municipalities; and other public and private community organizations such as churches, schools, and libraries." As the Court ruled in *Hudgens* v. *NLRB*, "a private entity who provides a forum for speech is not transformed by that fact alone into a state actor. [G]rocery stores put up community bulletin boards. Comedy clubs host open mic nights."

Nor did it matter that New York City had "designated MNN to operate the public access channels" or that "New York State heavily regulates MNN with respect to the public access channels. [That] the government licenses, contracts with, or grants a monopoly to a private entity does not convert the private entity into a state actor—unless the private entity is performing a traditional, exclusive public function."

Kavanaugh, J., dismissed an alternative contention that MNN was a state actor because it acted in the stead of New York City, which should be regarded as the owner or lessor of the public access channels under applicable New York law. "It does not matter that a provision in the franchise agreements between the City and Time Warner allowed the City to designate a private entity to operate the public access channels on Time Warner's cable system. [N]othing in the franchise agreements suggests that the City possesses any property interest in Time Warner's cable system, or in the public access channels on that system."

SOTOMAYOR, J., dissented: "New York City secured a property interest in public-access television channels when it granted a cable franchise to a cable company. State regulations require those public-access channels to be made open to the public on terms that render them a public forum. The City contracted out the administration of that forum to a private organization. [By] accepting that agency relationship, MNN stepped into the City's shoes and thus qualifies as a state actor.

"[The majority] is wrong in two ways. First, the majority erroneously decides the property question against the plaintiffs as a matter of law. [S]econd, and more fundamentally, the majority mistakes a case about the government choosing to hand off responsibility to an agent for a case about a private entity that simply enters a marketplace. [The] majority's opinion erroneously fixates on a type of case that is not before us: one [such as *Jackson*] in which a private entity simply enters the marketplace and is then subject to government regulation. [But] MNN is not a private entity that simply ventured into the marketplace. It occupies its role because it was asked to do so by the City, which secured the public-access channels in exchange for giving up public rights of way, opened those channels up (as required by the State) as a public forum, and then deputized MNN to administer them." The Court's reliance on prior public function cases was therefore misguided. "[When] the government hires an agent, [that agent is a state actor, regardless of whether the government] hired the agent to do something that can be done in the private marketplace too."

CHAPTER 12

LIMITATIONS ON JUDICIAL POWER AND REVIEW

■ ■ ■

2. STANDING

I. THE STRUCTURE OF STANDING DOCTRINE

P. 1755, at the end of note 6:

(c) The Court denied standing based on a causation analysis in CALIFORNIA v. TEXAS, 141 S.Ct. 2104 (2021), in which the plaintiffs argued that a change in law since the Court's prior cases involving the Affordable Care Act (ACA) rendered the statute facially invalid and therefore unenforceable. In *National Federation of Independent Business v. Sebelius*, 567 U.S. 519 (2012), Ch. 2, Sections 2 and 3, a divided Court held that Congress had no authority under the Commerce Clause to require individuals to purchase health insurance, but it upheld the individual mandate, which was enforced via a penalty payable to the Internal Revenue Service, as a valid exercise of the taxing power. After Congress subsequently reduced the penalty for non-purchase of insurance to $0, two individuals and a number of states sought invalidation of the entire ACA. According to the plaintiffs, the individual mandate could no longer be characterized as a tax, and all of the ACA's other provisions were so interconnected with the mandate that if the mandate was unconstitutional, the other provisions were not "severable" or separately enforceable.

Per BREYER, J., the Court found, by 7–2, that because none of the plaintiffs had standing to bring the action against the Secretary of Health and Human Services and the other defendant executive officials, it need not determine either the continuing validity of the now-unenforceable individual mandate or the severability of the mandate from the remainder of the ACA. Although the individual plaintiffs had alleged injury in the form of costs for the purchase of health insurance, they failed to satisfy the causation prong of the standing test: "Our cases have consistently spoken of the need to assert an injury that is the result of a statute's actual or threatened enforcement." In the absence of any credible threat that the defendants would enforce the mandate to purchase insurance, any harm that the plaintiffs had suffered when they bought insurance was not "fairly traceable" to the defendants.

Breyer, J., then turned to the claims of the plaintiff states, who had alleged that they suffered financial injuries from provisions of the ACA other than the individual mandate. In concluding that they lacked standing to challenge the mandate's validity, Breyer, J., again relied on causation principles. He dismissed the states' claim that the mandate led state residents to enroll in state-operated insurance programs that cost the states money by emphasizing the benefits that those programs provide. "[N]either logic nor intuition suggests that the presence of the minimal essential coverage requirement would lead an individual to enroll in one of those programs that its absence would lead them to ignore," he wrote, when the programs' benefits afforded another possible motive for their actions.

Breyer, J., acknowledged that provisions of the ACA other than the individual mandate imposed costs on the plaintiff states, including those incurred in providing information to residents and furnishing information to the Internal Revenue Service. But "no one" claimed that those other provisions, which "operate independently of" the individual mandate, violate the Constitution. The states' averments thus failed to establish standing to challenge the mandate, which they had not shown to be causally responsible for costs in complying with other provisions.

ALITO, J., joined by Gorsuch, J., dissented. "[T]he individual plaintiffs' claim to standing raise[d] a novel question," he thought, but it did not need to be addressed, since "the States have standing for reasons that are straightforward and meritorious." Alito, J., began his analysis of the states' standing with the premise that they had suffered financial injuries in complying with provisions of the ACA other than the individual mandate. Building on that premise, he further reasoned that if the states were correct (1) that the individual mandate was constitutionally invalid and (2) that other provisions of the ACA could not be severed from it, then the states' financial injuries were "indeed traceable to the mandate." According to Alito, J., the Court had granted standing to plaintiffs mounting facial challenges to statutes on grounds of statutory nonseverability in a number of prior cases and then treated the question of statutory severability as one to be resolved on the merits. That was the correct approach, he argued.

Breyer, J., did not respond the substance of Alito, J.'s, standing analysis, which he characterized as a "novel theory" that was neither argued by the plaintiffs in the lower courts nor presented in the plaintiffs' cert petitions and that "[w]e accordingly decline to consider." Thomas, J., filed a concurring opinion in which he agreed with and elaborated upon the "waiver" argument that Breyer, J., asserted more cryptically and that Alito, J., disputed.

Waiver arguments aside, Alito, J., appears correct that a number of the Court's prior decisions entertaining facial challenges to federal statutes have implicitly relied on a standing-though-nonseverability analysis under which plaintiffs who were directly harmed by one provision of a statute were permitted to argue for facial invalidation based on an alleged defect in another provision of an allegedly non-severable statute. (A recent example is *Seila Law LLC v. Consumer Financial Protection Bureau (CFPB)*, 140 S.Ct. 2183 (2020), Ch. 3 of this Supplement, in which a law firm that suffered harm pursuant to a statute's enforcement provisions was permitted to challenge another provision involving the appointment and removal of the CFPB's Director. Although the Court ultimately rejected the plaintiff's argument that an invalid limitation on presidential removal was not severable from the rest of the statute, it did so only after recognizing the plaintiff's standing to mount the facial challenge.) As Thomas, J., noted in his concurring opinion, however, "this Court has not addressed standing-through-inseverability in any detail, largely relying on it through implications."

When the Court more straightforwardly considers the soundness of the theory of "standing-through-inseverability," it will need to reckon with complex principles of severability and non-severability law that have often provoked sharp divisions among the Justices. For an introduction to some of the central concepts and their relationship to one another, see Richard H. Fallon, Jr., *Facial Challenges, Saving Constructions, and Statutory Severability*, 99 Tex.L.Rev. 215 (2020).

P. 1756, at the end of note 7:

Although courts will not order injunctive relief to redress "past" injuries that are unlikely to be repeated, UZUEGBUNAM v. PRECZEWSKI, 141 S.Ct. 792 (2021), held, per THOMAS, J., that a claim for nominal damages can suffice to establish standing and thus permit an adjudication of the merits of a plaintiff's constitutional claim. *Uzuegbunam* arose from a complaint that a public college and its officials violated the plaintiff's free speech rights to engage in religious proselytization on the college campus. By the time the case reached the Supreme Court, the college had withdrawn the policies that it enforced against Uzuegbunam, and Uzuegbunam was no longer a student at the college. Nonetheless, the Court held, by 8–1, that the plaintiff had alleged injury in fact, caused by the defendants, and that nominal damages would redress his injury: "By permitting plaintiffs to pursue nominal damages whenever they suffered a personal legal injury, the common law"—which provided relevant backdrop for the Court's interpretation of Article III— "avoided the oddity of privileging small-dollar economic rights over important, but not easily quantifiable, nonpecuniary rights."

ROBERTS, C.J., dissented, arguing that the common law cases clearly established only that plaintiffs could sue for nominal damages as a form of relief against ongoing or threatened future harms and that cases involving purely past injuries were different. He also thought that allowing nominal damages for past injuries conflicted with "modern justiciability principles" that authorize suit only when judicial relief will "compensat[e] the plaintiff for a past loss" or prevent "an ongoing or future harm."

P. 1757, after the second paragraph of note 9:

In *June Medical Services LLC. v. Russo*, 140 S.Ct. 2103 (2020), p. 35, *supra*, a divided Court allowed abortion doctors to assert the rights of their patients in challenging a statute that required any doctor who performs abortions to have admitting privileges at a nearby hospital. Dissenting, Alito, J., joined by Thomas and Gorsuch, JJ., argued that conflict-of-interest principles should bar the doctors' assertion of women's rights to challenge a statute ostensibly enacted to protect women's health.

II. CONGRESSIONAL POWER TO CREATE STANDING

P. 1766, at the end of note 2:

The Court clarified and arguably stiffened the "concrete" injury requirement in TRANSUNION LLC v. RAMIREZ, 141 S.Ct. 2190 (2021), another case under the Fair Credit Reporting Act (FCRA), which "requires consumer reporting agencies to 'follow reasonable procedures to assure maximum possible accuracy' in consumer reports and creates a cause of action for "any consumer" whose rights under the Act are violated. The TransUnion case grew out of a product marketed by a major credit reporting firm to alert its customers when consumers had names matching those on a U.S. government list of terrorists, drug traffickers, and other serious criminals. In determining which individuals to flag as "potential match[es]" with names on the government list, TransUnion initially conducted no investigation beyond a comparison of first and last names. Ramirez, who was misleadingly identified as a "potential match" and was rebuffed in his attempt to purchase a car as a result, sued TransUnion for failure to follow the "reasonable procedures" that FCRA requires. He also sought to certify a class of all 8,185 people to whom TransUnion sent a mailing during the period from January 1, 2011, to July 26, 2011, containing the information that their credit files contained alerts flagging them as possible terrorists or serious criminals. Within that seven-month period, however, TransUnion actually disseminated the potential-terrorist alerts with regard to only 1,853 consumers; although its files included alerts concerning 6,332 others, as well, it had not furnished those alerts to any customers within the seventh-month period subject to the parties' factual stipulations.

The Court, per KAVANAUGH, J., held by 5–4 that only the 1,853 individuals about whom false or misleading information was disseminated to TransUnion's customers suffered the "concrete" injury required for Article III standing. "The mere existence of a misleading alert in a consumer's internal credit file" did not constitute a concrete injury in the absence of publication or an analogue. Nor could standing be predicated on the risk that misleading information in the plaintiffs' credit files would be disseminated in the future. Although a risk of future injury will sometimes ground standing to seek injunctive relief, "in a suit for damages, the mere risk of future harm, standing alone, cannot qualify as a concrete harm—at least unless the exposure to the risk of future harm itself causes a separate concrete harm." The Court rejected the argument that credit reports on many of the 6,332 class members who claimed standing were likely sent to creditors outside of the seven-month period for which the parties had stipulated that only 1,853 of the plaintiffs' reports were actually distributed but within the nearly four-year period during which the plaintiffs claimed that TransUnion had violated their rights under FCRA. According to the Court, speculation about probabilities would not suffice; it was the plaintiffs' "burden to prove at trial that their reports were actually sent."

THOMAS, J., joined Breyer, Sotomayor, and Kagan, JJ., dissented. According to Thomas, J., Founding-era practice that informed the meaning of Article III drew a distinction between whether a plaintiff sued "based on the violation of a duty owed broadly to the whole community" or "asserts his or her own rights." Where a plaintiff sued to enforce a "public right" or a duty to the public as a whole, such as a general duty to obey or enforce the law, the existence of a justiciable case or controversy required a showing of concrete harm. But where a plaintiff sought to enforce a right or duty that was private or personal to her—such as a right to be free from trespass to her land—the plaintiff "needed only to allege the violation. [Courts] typically did not require any showing of actual damage."

In the case before the Court, each of the plaintiffs had "established a violation of his or her private rights," because all of the FCRA provisions under which they sued created "duties [that] are owed to individuals, not to the community writ large." By extending the demand for concrete harm to cases involving congressionally created private rights, Thomas, J., maintained, the Court had adopted an approach "remarkable in both its novelty and effects. Never before has this Court declared that legal injury is inherently insufficient to support standing."

"Even assuming that this Court should be in the business of second-guessing private rights," Thomas, J., thought that the plaintiffs had all pleaded concrete injuries: "[O]ne need only tap into common sense to know that receiving a letter identifying you as a potential drug trafficker or terrorist is harmful. All the more so when the information comes in the context of a credit report, the entire purpose of which is to demonstrate that a person can be trusted." According to Thomas, J., the errors in TransUnion's files created a real risk of disclosure at some time other than within the seven-month period in which TransUnion had disseminated erroneous credit reports involving roughly 25 percent of the plaintiff class. "Twenty-five percent over just a 7-month period seems, to me, 'a degree of risk sufficient to meet the concreteness requirement.'"

KAGAN, J., also filed a separate dissent, joined by Breyer and Sotomayor, JJ., to explain that she "differ[ed] with Justice Thomas on just one matter. * * * In his view, any 'violation of an individual right' created by Congress gives rise to Article III standing." By contrast, the Court had said in *Spokeo*, and she continued to believe, that "Article III requires a concrete injury even in the context of a statutory violation." Nevertheless, she thought that her view would lead to the same result as Thomas, J.'s "in all but highly unusual cases" due to the deference that the courts owed to Congress in determining "when something causes a harm or risk of harm in the real world."

3. TIMING OF ADJUDICATION

I. MOOTNESS

P. 1780, at the end of note 3:

In *New York State Rifle & Pistol Ass'n, Inc. v. City of New York*, 140 S.Ct. 1525 (2020), the Court ruled that a challenge to a New York City ordinance that barred licensed gun owners from transporting their weapons anywhere besides seven firing ranges within the City became moot after New York adopted an amended ordinance that allowed "direct[ ]" transport to and from other gun ranges and second homes. Dissenting, Alito, J., joined by Thomas and Gorsuch, JJ., maintained that because the amended ordinance continued to burden the petitioners' asserted right of "unrestricted access" to gun ranges, the dispute remained live.

In *Uzuegbunam v, Preczewski*, 141 S.Ct. 792 (2021), which arose from a public college's alleged violation of a student's First Amendment rights, the Court held that a claim for nominal damages of one dollar permitted adjudication on the merits even after the claim for injunctive relief became moot. Roberts, C.J., dissented. In the absence of either actual damages or ongoing harm, he thought that mootness doctrine applied.